Cooperation and Hierarchy in Ancient Bolivia

This book explores how past peoples navigated and created power structures and social relationships, using a case study from the Titicaca Basin of Bolivia (800 BC–AD 400). Based on the analysis of human skeletal remains, it combines anthropological social theory, archaeological contexts, and biological indicators of identity, disease, and labor to present a microhistory. The analysis moves in scale from individual experiences of daily life to broad patterns of shared identity and kinship during a time of significant economic and ecological change in the lake basin. The volume is particularly valuable for scholars and students interested in what bioarchaeology can tell us about power and social relationships in the past and how this is relevant to modern constructions of community.

Sara L. Juengst is an Associate Professor of Anthropology at the University of North Carolina at Charlotte, USA. As an anthropological bioarchaeologist, her research integrates social theory and skeletal evidence to address lived experiences of diet, disease, migration, and violence in the past and present. Sara's research primarily focuses on South America (Bolivia, Ecuador, and Peru), though she also participates in projects based in North Carolina, Kenya, and Nigeria. Her research explores how people navigated changing social and environmental climates, particularly highlighting how skeletons embody power and community.

Bodies and Lives
Series Editor: *Anna Osterholtz*

Bodies and Lives in Victorian England
Science, Sexuality, and the Affliction of Being Female
Pamela K. Stone and Lise Shapiro Sanders

Gender Violence in the American Southwest (AD 1100–1300)
Mothers, Sisters, Wives, Slaves
Debra L. Martin and Claira E. Ralston

Cooperation and Hierarchy in Ancient Bolivia
Building Community with the Body
Sara L. Juengst

www.routledge.com/Bodies-and-Lives/book-series/BODLIV

Cooperation and Hierarchy in Ancient Bolivia
Building Community with the Body

Sara L. Juengst

LONDON AND NEW YORK

First published 2023
by Routledge
4 Park Square, Milton Park, Abingdon, Oxon OX14 4RN

and by Routledge
605 Third Avenue, New York, NY 10158

Routledge is an imprint of the Taylor & Francis Group, an informa business

© 2023 Sara L. Juengst

The right of Sara L. Juengst to be identified as author of this work has been asserted in accordance with sections 77 and 78 of the Copyright, Designs and Patents Act 1988.

All rights reserved. No part of this book may be reprinted or reproduced or utilised in any form or by any electronic, mechanical, or other means, now known or hereafter invented, including photocopying and recording, or in any information storage or retrieval system, without permission in writing from the publishers.

Trademark notice: Product or corporate names may be trademarks or registered trademarks, and are used only for identification and explanation without intent to infringe.

British Library Cataloguing-in-Publication Data
A catalogue record for this book is available from the British Library

ISBN: 978-1-032-00470-9 (hbk)
ISBN: 978-1-032-00829-5 (pbk)
ISBN: 978-1-003-17597-1 (ebk)

DOI: 10.4324/9781003175971

Typeset in Sabon
by Newgen Publishing UK

To the Bolivian communities of the past and present—you have taught me more than I can say.

Contents

List of Figures		viii
List of Tables		xi
Acknowledgements		xii
List of Abbreviations		xiv
1	Studying Community and Power in the Past	1
2	Life in the Titicaca Basin	15
3	Daily Living: Sustenance, Stress, and Strain	36
4	Creating Relationships: Family and Friends	57
5	Growing Divisions: Violence and Identity	66
6	Building Community: Navigating New Terrain	82
	References	93
	Index	119

Figures

1.1	Map of the Copacabana Peninsula and relevant archaeological sites. Map drawn by Susan Brannock-Gaul	2
2.1	Lake Titicaca and surrounding landscape. Snowcapped peak is Illiampu	16
2.2	Modern fields with quinoa and other crops during the rainy season in 2018	20
2.3	Tortora reeds growing in the lake in summer 2012	21
2.4	Lakeside field with maize in spring 2018	22
2.5	Prehispanic terracing and Inka ruins on Isla del Sol (Isla Titicaca)	23
2.6	The reconstructed Yaya-Mama temple Ch'isi, with stone stelae in situ	25
2.7	The modern church at Sampaya, near the location of Muruqullu	30
2.8	Standing stone stelae at Kenasfena	31
3.1	Percent of burial samples displaying pathological lesions from each time period	42
3.2	Examples of pathological lesions from the Preceramic burials, including periosteal reactions on a tibia (A), osteomyelitis of a fibula (note the swollen and uneven appearance of the exterior surface) (B), and pitting on the posterior of a skull (C)	43
3.3	Percent of burial samples displaying osteoarthritic from each time period	44
3.4	Examples of osteoarthritis from the Preceramic burials, including lipping on the edges of lumbar vertebral bodies (A), pitting on the superior articular facets of the 2nd cervical vertebra (B), a Schmorl's node on the body of a lumbar vertebra (C), and pitting and lipping on the margin of a humeral head (D)	45

List of Figures   ix

3.5	Dietary isotopic results. Modern plant and animal samples with human mean values by time period. Human mean error bars are one standard deviation. (PC = Preceramic, EH = Early Horizon, EIP = Early Intermediate Period)	46
3.6	Distribution of average $\delta^{13}C$ apatite carbonate values for each time period compared to K-means cluster centroids for dietary estimation developed by Froehle et al. (2012). (PC = Preceramic, EH = Early Horizon, EIP = Early Intermediate Period; C1-C5 indicate the five clusters from Froehle et al. 2012)	47
3.7	Examples of pathological lesions from the Early Horizon burials, including periosteal reactions on a femur (A) and tibia (B), osteomyelitis on a radius (C), cribra orbitalia (D), porotic hyperostosis (E), and linear enamel hypoplasia (F)	49
3.8	Examples of osteoarthritis from the Early Horizon burials, including pitting and lipping on the margin of the lunar notch of an ulna (A), lipping and a Schmorl's node on a lumbar vertebra (B), and lipping on two lumber vertebral bodies (C)	50
3.9	Examples of pathological lesions from the EIP burials, including periosteal reactions on a tibia (A), osteomyelitis on a tibia (B), and pitting on the occipital bone of a juvenile individual (C)	53
3.10	Examples of osteoarthritis from the EIP burials, including pitting on the edge of the head of a radius (A), eburnation and pitting on the distal condyle of a femur (B), lipping and compression of a lumbar vertebra (C), and lipping and pitting on thoracic and lumbar vertebral bodies (D)	54
4.1	Predicted strontium map for Peru and Bolivia (adapted from Scaffidi and Knudson 2020)	61
4.2	Strontium isotope ratios for 40 sampled individuals. Black bar indicates the average minimum strontium ratio for the Titicaca Basin	64
5.1	Simplified types of cranial modification in the Andes. Top to bottom: unmodified, oblique, erect type 1, erect type 2	68
5.2	Percent of burial samples that displayed cranial modification for each time period	72

x List of Figures

5.3 Percent of burial samples that displayed skeletal trauma for each time period 73
5.4 Example of erect cranial modification from the Preceramic 73
5.5 Examples of skeletal trauma from the Preceramic, including healed sharp force trauma to the frontal bone (A) and a healed ulna fracture (B) 74
5.6 Examples of cranial modification from the Early Horizon. Top row: erect modification. Bottom row: oblique modification 76
5.7 Example of skeletal trauma from the Early Horizon, a perimortem fracture of the frontal of a juvenile individual 76
5.8 Examples of cranial modification from the EIP. Top row: erect modification. Bottom row: oblique modification 78
5.9 Examples of skeletal trauma from the EIP, including a perimortem cranial fracture and subsequent incomplete surgical intervention to remove piece of broken bone (A), an antemortem cranial fracture and healed subsequent surgical intervention (B), two healed rib fractures (C), and a healed ulnar fracture (D) 78

Tables

2.1	Chronology of the Titicaca Basin, associated material culture, and lake levels	17
2.2	Burial sample contributions from each site	28
2.3	Age estimates for the burial sample	33
2.4	Estimated sex of individuals in burial sample	35
3.1	Skeletal lesions of stress and disease by time period	41
3.2	Frequency of osteoarthritis at various joint surfaces	44
3.3	Mean isotope values by time period	46
4.1	Biodistance analysis where agreement equal to or above 0.5 indicates close correlation	63
5.1	Frequency of cranial modification types and trauma by time period	71
5.2	Connections between cranial modification and trauma by time period	72

Acknowledgements

First and foremost, thanks to the Bolivian communities of Copacabana, Chissi, Sampaya, Kollasuyu, Huayllani, Viluyo, and Belen who allowed the Yaya-Mama Project to excavate on their lands, permitted me to investigate the remains, and provided hospitality and guidance along the way, making this work possible in all ways.

Funding for the excavation of these remains was granted to Karen Mohr Chávez and Sergio Chávez from the National Geographic Society, Foundation for Research and Conservation of Andean Monuments, and Central Michigan University. Funding for the laboratory analyses in Bolivia and stable isotope analyses in the United States was provided by grants from the National Geographic Society, Sigma Xi, East Carolina University, the University of North Carolina at Chapel Hill, the University of North Carolina at Charlotte, and the Wenner-Gren Foundation.

Support for the conceptualization and performance of this research came from many fronts, including Dale Hutchinson, Sergio Chávez, Stanislava Chávez, Sara Becker, William Meyer, Meg Kassabaum, Amanda Thompson, Brian Billman, Margie Scarry, and Chris Weisen. Data collection in the lab in Copacabana was aided by David Hansen, Caitlin Homrich, Michael Zurek, Wren Wilson, Kelhi Henry, and Justin Miller. Isotope labwork and interpretation was made possible through the support of Drew Coleman, John Krigbaum, and Audrey Horne.

Writing was made possible through support from POMMLADSS featuring Scotti Norman, Lauren Kohut, Matt Velasco, Doug Smit, and Anna Guengerich, and SUAW featuring Letha Victor, Donna Lanclos, and Lydia Light. My colleagues at UNC Charlotte including Jon Marks, Lydia Light, and Nicole Peterson also provided invaluable feedback and edits.

Thanks to the editorial team at Routledge, especially Anna Osterholtz and Katherine Ong.

Acknowledgements xiii

Thanks to my American family and cheerleaders: Katherine Pinard, Eric Juengst, Laura Dorr, Chris Dorr, Sara C. Juengst, Maggie Juengst, Scout Juengst, and Faramir Juengst, and to my Bolivian family: Pablo Ramos, Juana Ramos, Rodrigo Ramos, Ariel Ramos, Estefani Ramos, Raymi Ramos, Maritza Gomez, and Nelly Gomez. I couldn't have done any of this without you.

Abbreviations

PC	Preceramic
EH	Early Horizon
EIP	Early Intermediate Period
CO	cribra orbitalita
PH	porotic hyperostosis
LEH	linear enamel hypoplasia
OA	osteoarthritis

1 Studying Community and Power in the Past

Humans organize their societies in many diverse ways, weaving complicated webs of kinship and belonging to share identities and create communities. While the nature of these relationships varies dramatically over time and space, humans tend to organize themselves in meaningful ways, delineating in- and out-groups, controlling and sharing access to key resources, and symbolically marking identities and social roles. And in doing so, we create communities and social relationships that structure many aspects of our lives, including with whom we interact, where we live, what we eat, what activities we participate in, and what types of power we wield or is wielded over us. Investigating community is therefore a vital way to understand how past peoples lived and how they experienced their social worlds.

This book pries and pokes into the past by investigating community and power for people living on the Copacabana Peninsula in the Titicaca Basin of modern-day Bolivia between 3000 BC and AD 400 (Figure 1.1). During this time, people domesticated plants and animals, built new villages, and created a shared religious tradition. All of these changes likely impacted daily life and altered the way people saw each other and themselves. However, these processes were not uniformly experienced by every person nor unidirectional—people manipulated their environments and their social relationships in various ways over time. This book therefore investigates variability in community and power in the same place over 3000 years. Moving in scale from individual experiences of daily life to broad patterns of shared identity and kinship, this book journeys into the Bolivian past to see how people navigated shifting currents of power against the dramatic backdrop of the high Andes.

2 Studying Community and Power in the Past

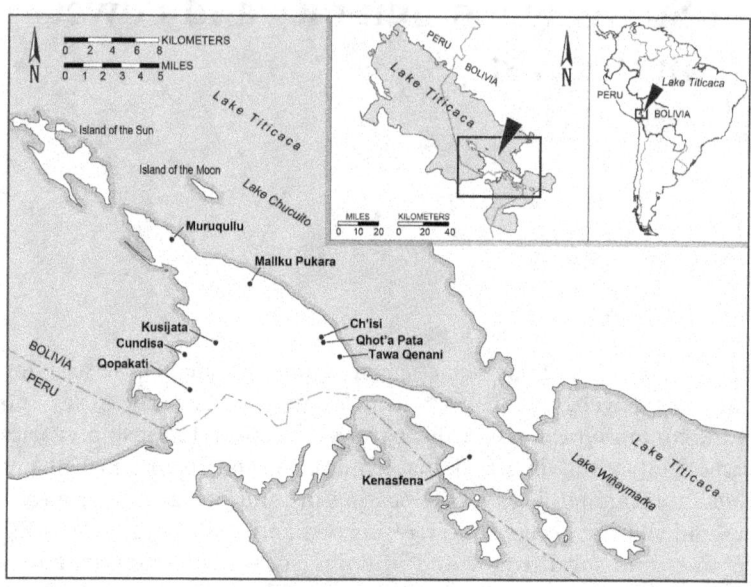

Figure 1.1 Map of the Copacabana Peninsula and relevant archaeological sites. Map drawn by Susan Brannock-Gaul.

In this book, the reader will explore different types of skeletal analysis in order to understand how power manifested in different ways on the Copacabana Peninsula of Bolivia over time. To get oriented, in Chapter 2, you will be introduced to the Titicaca Basin and the novel economic and ecological changes that occurred during the Preceramic Period (10,000–2000 BC), the Early Horizon (1000–50 BC) and the Early Intermediate Period (50 BC–AD 200). In the following three chapters (Chapters 3, 4, and 5), the book presents the bioarchaeological data that allows us to see the impact of these changes on three levels: (1) individual experiences with food, health, and labor; (2) shared experiences of biological kinship and migration; and (3) potentially divisive expressions and experiences of identity and violence. Finally, Chapter 6 integrates the lines of evidence presented in Chapters 3, 4, and 5, and suggests how social organization and power dynamics may have changed over time for Copacabana peoples. Chapter 6 also explores ways to apply these ideas to other archaeological contexts and modern day, addressing how knowing about power in the past can inform issues of modern importance.

What Makes a Community?

Communities broadly develop in two forms: natural and imagined communities. Natural communities are those formed or identified by proximity and daily interactions and are the most commonly recognized by archaeologists (Canuto and Yaeger 2000; Davis 2011; Marcus 2000). Studies of settlement patterns and subsistence strategies establish the existence of ancient natural communities. Because of close spatial proximity and shared material goods, people often relied upon each other to live their daily lives. However, "community is not [just] a spatial cluster of material remains" (Yaeger and Canuto 2000:12) but also includes temporally fleeting or materially invisible social relations and symbolic connections with people across long distances.

The phrase "imagined communities" refers to groups of people who identify with a deity, ancestor, belief system, or nation and see themselves as linked through this system (Anderson 1983; Isbell 2000). These communities can impact people as much as their physical proximity to other yet may be harder to trace archaeologically as they are defined by immaterial ties. Although these immaterial ideas are often "materialized" through iconography and artifacts, interpreting the artist's intent or what these shared artifacts mean is more difficult. Meaning and symbolism do not preserve as well as architecture and ceramics. To address this, Yaegar and Canuto (2000) suggest that we should consider communities as inherently social and continually emerging, but also requiring at least semi-frequent, co-presence of people in order to reinforce social bonds and re-establish community norms and practices. In this way, community is "both an institution that structures the practices of its members within defined spaces and the continually emergent product of that interaction" (Yaeger and Canuto 2000: 6).

Thus, we can move beyond the restrictive categories of natural and imagined communities, and define communities as networks which structure daily practice, form identities, and continually change. Importantly, the social relationships that form the bases of communities rely on power—shared, hoarded, or otherwise—to organize and maintain connections between people. Investigating multiple lines of evidence including geographic proximity, familial ties, symbolic relationships, and power disparities may provide the key to "unlocking" ancient communities.

Power in the Past

Throughout much of anthropology's history, anthropologists and archaeologists assumed most peoples, particularly those practicing agriculture, organized themselves competitively and hierarchically (i.e., Morgan 1877; Service 1962), with a limited number of people holding power over many others (i.e., Earle 1987; Fried 1967; Paynter 1989; although see Goldman 1910 for early ideas about the power of anarchy). Social theorists assumed the need for top-down vertical control, more a mirror to the social organization in which many social theorists and archaeologists lived than an objective truth (Appadurai 1988; Borck 2019; Henry et al. 2017). In actuality, human societies organize in numerous ways, including systems of cooperation, heterarchy, and anarchy, modes of organization increasingly recognized since the incorporation of postmodern, feminist, and queer theories into anthropology and archaeology (Angelbeck and Grier 2012; Blackmore 2011; Crumley 1995; DeMarrais 2016; Engelstad 1991; Franklin 2001; Graeber and Wengrow 2021; Levy 2012; Spencer-Wood 2010; others). Moreover, it is clear that nuance exists within these varied systems, with no direct correlation between type of political organization (i.e., state) and manner of dispersing power (i.e., hierarchy). In other words, it would be incorrect to assume complex social systems necessitate hierarchy or coercive control, and vice versa.

Cooperation is a form of human interaction that is likely deeply rooted and often more useful than working individually (Coelho and McClure 2016; Mead 1937; Stanish 2017). Mead (1937:8) defines cooperation as "the act of working together to one end" and cooperative relationships have been at the center of many ethnographic accounts of small-scale communities and nation-building attempts (Anderson 1983; Mead 1937). Despite the ubiquity of cooperation to human groups over time and space, it is identified less often than competition or coercion, forms of organization that may involve certain parties holding power over or attempting to wrest power from others (DeMarrais et al. 1996). Material and physical signatures of cooperation may be more difficult to observe; or, it is possible that archaeologists have tended to see patterns similar to their own social circumstances rather than capturing the true range of possibilities (Borck 2018).

Hierarchy exists in varied and nuanced ways, arising in many parts of the world in response to various stimuli, including increasing sedentism and agriculture (i.e., Price and Bar-Yosef 2010), exclusive ritual knowledge (i.e., Aldenderfer 2010; Earle 1997; Flannery and

Marcus 2012), climate crises (i.e., Kyle and Reitsema 2020), and intrusion of other cultures and colonial powers (i.e., Hu and Quave 2020; Wang and Marwick 2020; Wernke 2012). While other systems of power also involve inequality, hierarchy necessarily involves the creation and maintenance of social inequality and ranked social classes (Price and Feinman 2010). The means of maintaining power vary between hierarchies but often involve some level of coercive control and apparent competition between groups, to keep people with less power from demanding more. Within hierarchies, access to wealth, health, controlled substances, elite goods, and deities have been used to generate and maintain power. These various systems may have archaeological correlates, particularly reflecting elite status and inequality (Drennan and Dai 2010; Klaus et al. 2017) although interpreting these signatures is rarely simple (Trigger 1999).

Heterarchy differs from hierarchy in that it is built on elements that are unranked in relation to each other or ranked in various nonlinear ways (Crumley 1979, 1987, 2007). This often means that power is shared or deployed by different groups at different times, depending on their expertise or situation at hand. Importantly, no single group or person dominates the rest. For example, the system of checks and balances present in many government systems prevents any one governmental branch from dominating the others, while still allocating power to those individual branches over certain subjects (i.e., legislature, judiciary, etc.). Heterarchy can vary by scale and time, producing different power relationships between individuals, communities, or other groups of people that shift in power depending on material, topic, etc. In fact, heterarchy and hierarchy are often in flux, as power circulates through networks of people and places (Crumley 1995, 2007; Spencer-Wood 2010). Heterarchy appears different archaeologically as it is often not associated with the accumulations of wealth and health commonly found with stratification (although notable health exceptions exist). Scholars have identified past heterarchy and societies with decentralized power networks based on careful analysis of site size, settlement patterns, wealth distribution, and social network analysis (Crumley 1995, 2007; Kristiansen 2010; Levy 1995, 2012; Spencer-Wood 2010).

Anarchy is social organization that explicitly rejects dominating or coercive control, but instead relies on individual and cooperative acts (Angelbeck et al. 2018; Goldman 1910). Anarchy differs from heterarchy in that an anarchy lacks a central governing force altogether, whereas a heterarchy still uses organized governance, albeit without power concentrated in one group or individual. Anarchies (i.e., societies without a central governing force) are regularly identified in the past, if not explicitly labeled as such. Approaching interpretations of past societies from an anarchism framework is thus an important way to understand decentralized networks and social organizations (Angelbeck and Grier 2012; Borck and Sanger 2017).

Archaeologists can identify material correlates of power, and strategies people have used to promote cooperative or competitive relationships, providing important regional context for social organization. Identifying hierarchy often takes the form of unequal distribution of mortuary goods, varying household sizes, differential access to rare or exotic resources, and quality and quantity of domestic artifacts. For example, hierarchy was clearly identified at a Late Bronze Age site in Cyprus based on variable tomb size and location, and inclusion of grave goods, a trend which elaborated over time as the area urbanized (Keswani 1989). Increasingly, archaeologists are identifying non-hierarchical modes of social organization and power as well. Cooperation, consensus, anarchy, and heterarchy are also visible archaeologically through settlement pattern, distribution of goods and resources, and access to ritual space. For instance, based on distribution of fortifications and ethnographic accounts of anarchy, it is clear that coastal Salish groups in Northwest North America were able to successfully balance decentralized social organization and broad-scale communal alliances during times of conflict over the last 1600 years (Angelbeck 2016). Similarly, Rautman (2016) interprets circular villages in the American Southwest as both a sign of cooperative ideology and an expression of in-group solidarity, expressly denoting those outside the circle as other. Both of these studies use architectural analyses to demonstrate consensus and cooperation amid anarchical or dispersed social organization. Heterarchy is also identifiable archaeologically through site size and distribution, production and distribution of ceramics and tools, and connections between communities (Crumley 1995). Levy (1995) clearly demonstrates this in an analysis of Bronze Age Denmark, using settlement pattern and gender iconography to show that households engaged in lateral and vertical systems of power, navigating heterarchy and hierarchy in different contexts. Through these various methods, archaeologists are able to untangle complex social dynamics to reveal the choices people made about power and collaboration over time.

However, archaeological analyses of power rely on group-level material culture and settlement patterns, leaving out individuals' nuanced experiences. Investigating power on a small scale is also important to reconstructing past social organizations, particularly when

Studying Community and Power in the Past 7

considering decentralized networks and nuanced social relationships as individual choices and identities may play pivotal roles in these strategies. Human skeletal remains provide an opportunity to see this smaller scale, as they reflect individual experiences throughout the life course. Thus, this book investigates multiple scales of power, moving between individuals, their communities, and broader social organization to see how people navigated changing circumstances over time.

Learning About Community and Power from Bones

Bioarchaeology provides means to investigate an individual's life history, and as a part of that, their experiences with power and their community. Social structures associated with status impact people's biology, as daily lives, access to resources, mobility, cultural identities, and social interactions become embodied and inscribed on bodies and skeletons in various ways (i.e., Bourdieu 1977; Sofaer 2006). While the exact structures and policies vary, each of these larger social processes may change the risk and experience of stress and disease, access to resources, ability to move across the landscape, trauma experiences, labor, and cultural body modifications which are linked with power relationships (i.e., Goodman and Martin 2002; Klaus et al. 2017; Martin and Harrod 2015).

Studying human remains is not without controversy. Skeletons can provide an important record of lived experiences because they are the physical remains of once living peoples, who were interred by their kin and communities in specific ways and places. Excavating and studying burials is thus not a practice to be taken lightly (Walker 2008; Zuckerman et al. 2014). Bioarchaeologists need to consider the cultural, social, and political contexts in which they work and from which the human remains come, in order to minimize risk and harm to living or past peoples. In doing so, researchers can employ an ethical and culturally-relevant framework focused on "deriving *meaning from* and creating *meaning for* human remains" (Zuckerman et al. 2014: 514). In this research, human remains were excavated, analyzed, and photographed with permission of local descendant communities and as a part of a larger collaborative archaeological project committed to local engagement and education (discussed more in Chapter 2). These communities were part of the conversation about the research from the conception of the project through analysis and publication. Consent for publication of photographs of human remains was given by descendant communities around the Copacabana Peninsula and isotope samples were exported to the United States in 2006 with permission from the National Institute of Archaeology in Bolivia (NIAR).

While many experiences of power are recorded in bone, human skeletons do not perfectly capture every aspect of life. Severe disease or starvation may cause death before diagnostic skeletal lesions can actually form, complicating bioarchaeological interpretations (DeWitte and Stojanowski 2015; Wood et al. 1992). Individuals who do present skeletal and dental lesions may have thus been more resilient over the long term, surviving disease episodes and nutritional deficiencies for long enough that the skeleton could react, while those without lesions may have been weaker immunologically and succumbed to disease or malnutrition prior to lesions formation. This "osteological paradox" thus presents interpretive challenges for bioarchaeologists, as those without lesions may have been either the healthiest (albeit still dead) or the most stressed, while those with lesions lay somewhere in between. It is thus important to investigate multiple indicators across the skeleton and include as much archaeological context and chronological control as possible (DeWitte and Stojanowski 2015; Goodman and Martin 2002; Temple and Goodman 2014).

Stress, Diet, Disease, and Skeletal Lesions

Patterns of health and disease often reflect social hierarchy and community boundaries. In fact, poor health may be the most reliable indicator of low social status in the majority of circumstances for many reasons including: increased workload of lower social classes, substandard housing, limited access to clean water or good sanitation practices, psychosocial stress caused by discrimination and worry, increased exposure to violence, and decreased access to nutrition (Goodman 1998; Goodman and Martin 2002; Marquez Morfin 1998; Sapolsky 2004). These contributors to health are not individual choices but structured by larger processes such as public policies, systems of exchange, subsistence strategies, and social roles (see de la Cova 2012; Farmer 1999, 2003; Goodman 1998; Shuler 2011; Swedlund and Ball 1998). While the type of structures and policies in place are variable by time and space, these larger processes leave people at increased *risk* of negative health outcomes.

Disease and nutritional status, both of which are often dictated by social roles such as gender or class, are inextricably linked and directly impact each other (McDade et al. 2008; Scrimshaw 2003; Scrimshaw et al. 1959). Depending on one's nutritional status and access to resources in order to replenish bodily stores of energy, supplementary bodily resources may or may not be available. In addition to bodily reserves, certain key nutrients (i.e., iron, vitamin C, vitamin A) help build the cells that identify and fight pathogens and are thus integral to maintaining immune function. Caloric intake overall is also necessary for adequate immune function as the immune system is energetically costly. Without key minerals such as iron or important vitamins, or an overall adequate caloric intake, immune function can be negatively impacted and an individual who has only adequate nutrition may not be able to supplement bodily resources used by intense or prolonged physical activity (Goodman and Leatherman 1998; Scrimshaw 2003).

Cyclically, when one is ill, they are less likely to absorb important vitamins and minerals or to acquire adequate nutrition. Immune stimulation and fighting infection actually limits uptake of nutrients, as energy is diverted to other systems. And, the symptoms of disease may contribute to loss of nutrients directly, through vomiting, blood loss, or diarrhea. Cultural practices surrounding illness often proscribe strict dietary regimens for those that are ill and may or may not include nutrients necessary to rebound from disease. This can create a cycle of illness and malnutrition, especially during childhood when bodily growth already puts a premium on energy (McDade et al. 2008; Scrimschaw et al. 1959).

Thus, patterns of health and disease can reflect social structures and hierarchies present in a population by showing who has access to nutritional resources and who is at risk of disease. Status hierarchies may be evidenced by lesions patterns in particular, as elite individuals eat different diets, perform different activities, live in different locations, and interact less regularly with non-elites. Repetitive long-term stressors, such as chronic malnutrition, disease, and intense labor, are visible on human skeletal and dental remains through a variety of skeletal and dental lesions. In Chapter 3, this book shows how observing differences in prevalence of lesions and indicators associated with stress between burial populations can demonstrate differences in health and subsequently, differences in social status.

Food, Symbolism, and Diet

Access to desired or special food items is directly linked to status. Foods are often highly symbolic, tied to social status, and/or associated with ritual settings or specific locales, meanings which are reinforced through consumption practices at sacred places or at particular times (see Berryman 2010; Feeley-Harnik 1995; Mintz and Du Bois 2002; Parker Pearson 2003). Through these repetitive acts, certain foods become central to and necessary for ritual practices and maintenance of particular identities, and people holding those identities are more likely to consume a sacred food item in significant contexts and potentially in greater volume than other communities' members (especially if it is otherwise limited or exotic). Participants in traditions who consume certain foods are thus delineated from non-participants, a division which is reinforced every time that food is consumed. (Berryman 2010; Mintz and Du Bois 2002). Because of this division, analyzing differential consumption of food and highly valued food items in particular can reveal community and ritual and/or status affiliations.

Skeletons allow us to see what was eaten through stable isotope analyses of carbon ($^{13}C/^{12}C$) and nitrogen ($^{15}N/^{14}N$), elements linked to the types of food we eat (Ambrose 1993; Schoeninger and Moore 1992, and others). When we eat certain types of plant foods, their carbon isotopes are incorporated into human skeletons and dentition. Similarly, protein sources vary in nitrogen based on trophic level, and are subsequently incorporated into bone. Thus, these isotopes can show us what types of foods were consumed on average during a person's childhood (from teeth) and later in life (from bones). Explored more fully in Chapter 3, stable isotopes can help us understand broad patterns of the type of foods consumed, and who had access to what resources.

Labor and Osteoarthritis

Physical labor varies with power. In hierarchical settings, the heaviest loads are often placed on the literal shoulders of those without power (Goodman and Leatherman 1998; Larsen 1995; Shuler 2011). However, in cooperative or anarchical labor strategies, labor may be evenly distributed as people collaborate to achieve tasks or divide work in more equitable ways that do not result in certain individuals being more heavily taxed than others. In heterarchical settings, patterns of activity might map differently and appear varied between individuals, perhaps related to neighborhood or ethnic group performing different but complementary tasks (Becker 2017).

Human skeletons record labor in several ways: through overall wear and tear on the skeleton in the form of osteoarthritis (OA) and degenerative joint diseases, through the impact of muscle development and attachment to bones, and through the overall form and shape of long bones (Becker 2017, 2020; Bridges 1991, 1992; Jurmain et al. 2011; Schrader 2019; Shuler 2011; Waldron 2019). These markers do not necessarily record activities perfectly, as many factors may impact

Studying Community and Power in the Past   11

the development of muscles and degenerative joint problems; however, highly repetitive tasks or movements are often identifiable as biomechanical forces are continually placed upon the bones and joints (Jurmain et al. 2011; Schrader 2019).

Kinship and Biodistance

Community structures are often related to ancestry and reproductive relationships. Kinship systems and family are fundamental to human societies, helping to teach cultural values and daily practices to the young, and often organizing economic relationships, and have thus been central to anthropological studies over time (i.e., Deloria 1944; Evans-Pritchard 1951; Fei 1939; Malinowski 1913; Mead 1934). However, what counts as kinship takes many diverse forms and include biological descent, affinal and consanguinal relationships, and other types of fictive kin (Johnson and Paul 2016; Levi-Strauss 1983; Meyer et al. 2012; Sahlins 2013).

While kinship is not always genetic, the biological needs of human infants necessitate extended and intimate parenting, which often creates strong ties between parents and offspring. Social relationships surrounding parenting and extended families often create the basis for community membership. Thus, genetic relationships expressed in phenotype can help archaeologists recreate one aspect of community, given that community members are often both social and biological kin (Johnson and Paul 2016; Meyer et al. 2012; Stojanowski and Buikstra 2004; Stojanowski and Schillaci 2006). While measuring phenotypic expression of genetic relationships is not a perfect measure of community, it can be the first step to outlining social relationships, especially when combined with markers of social affiliation such as burial location and associated material goods. Chapter 4 presents biodistance analysis as a way to understand the genetic and biological relationships between individuals, as one way to access kinship.

Mobility, Proximity, and Heavy Isotopes

While physical proximity is certainly not the only delineation of communities, the idea of "natural communities" relies heavily on proximity. People that live near each other often engage in trade as a way to access necessary food items and other material goods. Along with material goods, these relationships can also contribute to the trade of ideas, practices, and beliefs. Modern potters in the northern Titicaca Basin regularly trade with neighboring towns as they all have become experts in one or two steps of the potting process, that is, clay collection, molding forms, firing large/small pots, and decoration. While each village maintains a local identity, they are closely linked to their neighbors to form a larger potting community (Chávez, K. 1992).

Individual mobility is often limited by power; those with more power may be able to move more readily, or have others transplanted at their discretion. For instance, the Inka Empire regularly relocated large portions of conquered communities, in order to weaken social ties and manipulate labor (Covey 2000, 2006; others). Under the control of some Andean states, Wari, Tiwanaku, and Moche, people moved around considerable regions, as they created colonies, expanded into new areas, and developed elaborate trade networks (Goldstein 2003; Knudson 2004; Knudson and Tung 2011). Finally, during times of war, people were occasionally captured and brought to sacred locations to be sacrificed or held captive (Sutter and Cortez 2005; Sutter and Verano 2006). Sometimes people who were buried near each other may have lived or originated from much further away and relocated either through force or choice.

Bioarchaeology can test geographic relationships of past peoples through strontium isotope studies. Strontium naturally varies according to the age of local geology and this mineral becomes incorporated into the skeleton over one's lifetime. Testing and comparing the strontium signatures in bone and teeth of individuals and populations can show where people lived prior to their deaths (Ericson 1985; Kundson 2004; Price et al. 2002; Slovak and Paytan 2011). In Chapter 4, the book explores how movement of peoples within the Titicaca Basin may have created new types of communities over time.

Identity and Body Modification

Cultural body modification is often linked to power and group demarcation, as people physically alter bodies to mark identity and belonging (i.e., Atkinson 2002; Berger et al. 2019; Blom 2005a; DeMello 2000; Geller 2004; Klesse 1999; Stone 2012; Stone and Sanders 2020; Te Awekotuko 2003). These practices can take a variety of forms, including the physical molding of the head and feet into various desired shapes, body decoration in the form of paint or tattooing, hairstyles conveying occupation and status, and inlaying precious metals into teeth, among others. Highly visible and unchangeable forms of modification permanently mark some aspect of one's identity, and rapidly communicate that with anyone who sees and interprets the signal.

Studying Community and Power in the Past 13

In South America, modified crania, face-painting, hairstyles, and dental decorations gave symbolic power to those modified and identified these individuals as belonging to certain groups (Blom 2005a, 2005b; Juengst et al. 2021; Torres-Rouff 2002, 2008; Vasquez de Arthur 2018; Velasco 2018; others). Skeletally, South American body modification can be observed through practices such as cranial and dental modification. These permanent markers of identity, in life and observable after death, were often tied to gender roles, ethnic group, and social status (i.e., Blom 2005a, 2005b; Torres-Rouff 2002, 2008; Torres-Rouff and Knudson 2017; Velasco 2018). Chapter 5 presents rates and types of cranial modification in particular, in order to see if these identity indicators were linked to other lived experiences, such as trauma.

Violence and Trauma

Violence and trauma are other valuable lines of bioarchaeological inquiry to understand status and power. Skeletal injury may result from accidents or moments of intentional violence, caused by a range of behaviors, including both socially sanctioned and external violence (Martin et al. 2012; Walker 2001, and others). Violence is often tied to ideological and social control and usually not equally distributed across society. Not limited to warfare or large-scale conflict, violence may permeate daily life through socially sanctioned targeting of certain individuals or ethnic groups, through social structures that put some at higher risk of violence and disease than others, or through ritualized violence such as cannibalism or ritual fights, as clearly shown in this forum's study of Wari peoples. The visual impact of broken bodies (living and dead) is culturally dependent but has been used as a way to manipulate the living and reinforce power relationships (Crandall and Martin 2014; Tung 2014).

Violent conflict also happens outside of "normal" social bounds and often increases during times of changing sociopolitical relationships and environmental stress. In these cases, larger scale violence such as warfare and systemic raiding may occur. However, even in chaotic violent landscapes, violence is not random. Certain groups (typically those with less power) are generally targeted as victims of violence (Martin et al. 2012; Walker 2001, and others). Low-status individuals can be targets for violence in instances of daily structural violence, socially sanctioned punishment, and episodes of large-scale war.

Different patterns of skeletal injury can be used to reveal the experiences that produced these traumatic lesions (Walker 2001). For instance, face-to-face conflicts often result in trauma to the facial or frontal bones, while injuries to the posterior portion of the skull may occur while fleeing an attacker. Arm fractures, particularly on the ulna, are associated with defensive gestures, such as raising an arm to ward off a blow. Sharp force or penetrating trauma can imply the use of a weapon, suggesting intentional violence rather than an accident. Conversely, wrist and leg fractures may suggest accidental falls, rather than intentional harm and armed conflict (although also not mutually exclusive). Explored in Chapter 5, the location and type of fractures distinguish between accidental and violent trauma, and patterns of violence are observed for individuals and the population more broadly.

Integration and Interpretation

Given these various lines of evidence, how might one assess them to see power and social organization? Hierarchy and competition may leave telltale signs of ranked inequality through unorthodox burials and reproductive exclusion of certain groups, disproportionate distribution of fractured bones and extensive pathological lesions, and marked body modifications, emphasizing in-group membership. More subtle power disparities may be visible through lesions of systemic stress and limited access to resources for certain people within larger groups. Identifying instances of cooperation (outside of hierarchy or within larger hierarchical complexes), anarchy, and heterarchy is also possible through careful assessment of these lesions when disparities are not present or variable across individuals. By using a combination of methods, bioarchaeologists gain insight into both childhood and adult immuno-nutritional insults, labor patterns, risk of intentional violent trauma, family dynamics, cultural identities, and movement and migration, allowing identification of patterns of cooperative resource use, violence, and identity. While cultural contexts vary across time and space, the embodied experiences of power are still identifiable.

2 Life in the Titicaca Basin

Lake Titicaca is the world's highest navigable lake at 3,810 m above sea level (Figure 2.1). People have lived in this part of the world for at least 10,000 years and today, the lake is divided geopolitically between Peru and Bolivia and supports many local agricultural and pastoral communities. The lake also draws many domestic and international tourists; the large, flat lake surface, surrounding snowy mountain peaks and rolling hills, and series of islands throughout the lake create a unique, picturesque landscape with many opportunities for hiking and boating. This chapter presents the environment, wildlife, and history of human occupation of the Titicaca Basin to introduce the reader to the natural and social variables that humans have faced while living there.

Ecology and Environment of the Titicaca Basin

The climate of the lake basin is an interesting feature of the region as it crosses several ecological categories. Technically located in an intertropical climactic zone, the high altitude and mountainous terrain keep ambient temperatures and humidity low for much of the year. The rainy season is short, between December and March, and the extended dry season from April to November provide endless sunny days and cool nights. (Although, global climate change is shifting this pattern, with rain lingering through June in recent years.)

The Copacabana Peninsula splits the lake into two parts, united only by the thin Straits of Tiquina. The northern portion of the lake, called Chucuito or Lago Grande, is larger and deeper, containing numerous small islands and draining into marshy swamps, especially on the southeastern border. The southern portion of the lake is called Wiñaymarka or Lago Pequeño and is overall smaller, shallower, and with fewer islands. These lakes may have been fully separated

DOI: 10.4324/9781003175971-2

16 Life in the Titicaca Basin

Figure 2.1 Lake Titicaca and surrounding landscape. Snowcapped peak is Illiampu. Photo by author.

during extremely cold periods of the Pleistocene, as lake water become trapped in glaciers.

The smaller, shallower portion of the lake is more susceptible to climactic shifts and has undergone several periods of significant water level change. In fact, over the last 10,000 years, the lake has gone through a series of lake level changes, mostly in response to long-term droughts (Table 2.1) (Abbott et al. 1997; Baker et al. 2005; Capriles et al. 2016; Weide et al. 2017). These cycles of relatively high or stable water levels (1500–800 BC; 200 BC–AD 100; AD 350–1100) and low water levels (600–400 BC; AD 100–350; AD 1100–1400) had significant impacts for human settlements as they posed different challenges and opportunities for subsistence (Capriles et al. 2016; Juengst et al. 2021; Miller et al. 2010).

Despite fluctuations in lake level, both areas of the lake support similar biomass and share many aquatic species. The lake and lake basin are home to diverse species of fish, amphibian, reptile, bird, and mammal, in addition to supporting diverse flora adapted to living at such high altitude. The lake has significant effects for the regional

Table 2.1 Chronology of the Titicaca Basin, associated material culture, and lake levels

Absolute Chronology	Relative Chronology	Titicaca Basin Chronology	Associated Culture	Lake Levels (based on lake cores)
AD 1540–1800	Colonial Period (COL)	Colonial Period	Spanish	Very High
AD 1450–1540	Late Horizon (LH)	Late Horizon	Inka	High
AD 1100–1450	Late Intermediate Period (LIP)	Altiplano/Pacajes Period	Lupaka and Colla	Low
AD 500–1100	Middle Horizon (MH)	Middle Horizon	Tiwanaku	High
AD 1–500	Early Intermediate Period (EIP)	Late Formative Period	"Late" Yaya-Mama	Very Low AD 100–350
1000 BC–AD 1	Early Horizon (EH)	Early and Middle Formative Period	"Early" Yaya-Mama	Fluctuating: High 1000–600BC, Low 600–400 BC, High 400 BC–AD1
3000–1000 BC	Late (Cotton) Preceramic VI	Initial Period	Viscachani	Very High

ecology, raising lakeside temperatures by as much as 8°C and providing habitats for a variety of plant, fish, amphibian, and avian species (Stanish 2003; Miller et al. 2010).

The majority of fish in the lake belong to two genera: *Orestias* (common name, killifish) and *Trichomycterus* (common name, burrowing catfish). There are 26 species within these two genera, most of which are relatively small in size, ranging 5–19 cm in length (Miller et al. 2010). The Orestias species are fairly diverse and adapted to a range of local niches throughout the lake, while the Trichomycterus species tend to be bottom dwellers feeding on organic remains and macro-invertebrates along the lake floor. Today, other species such as rainbow trout and silverside have been introduced to the lake, outcompeting some indigenous fish and decimating their populations. The native species are still commercially fished but are less valuable than the newly introduced species (Orlove 2002).

Amphibious life in the lake includes many species of toad and frog, including one of the largest frog species in the world, Telmatobius coleus or the Titicaca frog. While these frogs are impressive, weighing as much as two pounds and stretching more than 20 inches long, they mostly dwell on the lake floor, absorbing oxygen directly through their thin, wrinkled skin, and are rarely seen today (Navas 1997). More common are smaller varieties of toad and frog which also inhabit the lake. While not eaten today, they are occasionally found in archaeological assemblage, suggesting that they were consumed in the past (Moore et al. 1999).

Waterfowl and terrestrial lakeside birds are plentiful with over 60 species residing on or near the lake today. Archaeologically, at least 23 taxa have been identified at just one site (Moore et al. 1999), indicating that this high level of diversity is traceable into the past. Bird varieties include aquatic birds such as coots, grebes, ducks, flamingos, cormorants, and Andean geese, in addition to more terrestrial birds such as tinamous, doves, flickers, owls, and Andean sparrows (Moore et al. 1999; Janusek 2008). Three of these types (large grebes, cormorants, and the ruddy duck) are present in the archaeological record but have not been observed in the region since 1996 (Moore et al. 1999). Many of these birds build nests in accessible places along the edge of the lake, adding to the resource base exploited by humans in the past and present.

Mammalian life in the lake basin can be divided into two main groups: large mammals which include camelids, deer, and predators, and small mammals which are mostly rodents. Camelids (llamas, alpacas, vicuñas, and guanacos) have been present in the region for at least 10,000 years, with domestication of llamas and alpacas occurring between 3000 BC and 1500 BC (Aldenderfer 1989; Moore 2011, 2016). These species have a fairly important impact on the local ecology as they need significant sources of food and water to maintain their large herds (Dransart 2002; Moore et al. 1999). Regularly found at archaeological sites and herded today, the domesticated camelids are and were used for meat, for transporting goods long distances, and as a source for wool and bone tools (Moore et al. 1999; Moore et al. 2007; Stanish 2003). Vicuña and guanacos are extremely rare, if ever present, in the lake basin today but may have been hunted in the past. Highland deer are also rare in the modern day but were hunted by early Titicaca Basin residents (Aldenderfer 1989). Large mammals in this region also include predators such as pumas, Andean wolves, Andean foxes, and small felines called titis. These predators are increasingly rare but have been found archaeologically. The felines were in fact often depicted in ancient iconography (Chávez, K. 1988; Chávez, S. 1992, 2002, 2004; Moore et al. 1999). Small mammals native to the lake basin include mice, *viscacha* (the guinea pig's wild cousin), and guinea pig or *cuy*.

Archaeology of the Titicaca Basin

The lake basin has been home to many sociopolitical groups over the past 10,000 years, including the first state in the southern Andes, Tiwanaku. The archaeological record shows the various ways people navigated their world and demonstrates change over time in how people survived and thrived in the lake basin. Using a general Andean chronology (Table 2.1), here I briefly summarize the social and economic changes of the last 10,000 years.

During the Preceramic Period (10,000–2000 BC), Titicaca Basin groups were generally mobile. These foragers hunted wild deer and camelids, utilized lake resources, and gathered wild crops. As the name implies, these people did not create ceramics. Most archaeological sites excavated to date were likely hunt camps, indicating intermittent travel throughout the lake basin and into lower regions on a regular basis (Capriles et al. 2016; Haas and Viviano Llave 2015). Wild game from land and lake comprised most of Preceramic diets (Capriles et al. 2016; Juengst et al. 2021) but wild tubers and other grains also played an important role (Watson and Haas 2017). It is also likely that archery technology was invented during this period, expanding the range and types of wild game available (Kitchell et al. 2021). This mixed use of wild resources shifted over time, and by the end of the Preceramic Period, people in the Titicaca Basin herded domesticated camelids, in addition to gathering wild plants, lake resources, and

Figure 2.2 Modern fields with quinoa and other crops during the rainy season in 2018. Photo by author.

hunting highland deer (Aldenderfer 1989). Surprisingly robust and tall (Juengst et al. 2017a), these individuals successfully used the landscape and available resources and were well adapted to living in this region.

By the Initial Period (2000–1000 BC) and into the Early Horizon (1000–50 BC), household-level cultivation of plants combined with foraging, hunting, herding, and fishing allowed for the establishment of semi to fully sedentary settlements (Bandy 2004; Bruno and Whitehead 2003; Capriles et al. 2014; Hastorf 2005; Moore et al. 1999). Some of these first plant domesticates included quinoa (*Chenopodium quinoa*), canihua (*Chenopodium pallidicaule*), potato (*Solanum tuberosum*), and oca (*Oxalis tuberosum*), plants that continue to be grown today (Figure 2.2) (Bruno and Whitehead 2003; Chávez 2004; Miller et al. 2021). Animal domesticates included the aforementioned camelids (alpacas and llamas) and potentially cuy. Wild animals such as guanacos, fish, and birds were also regularly consumed (Moore et al. 1999; Moore et al. 2007).

While llamas and alpacas had been almost certainly been domesticated by this time period, how they were used is less certain. It remains unclear whether camelids were domesticated as a meat resource or for their other by-products, including wool, bone, and dung (Moore et al. 1999). Camelid remains recovered from the site of Chiripa dating to the Initial Period are mostly from large species (llama or guanaco), which is similar to data from modern herding groups in southern Peru, who primarily use their animals for meat. However, most of the camelid remains from the Initial Period were from adult or older juvenile animals, which is in stark contrast to the Peruvian samples composed mainly of juveniles (Kent 1982; Moore et al. 1999). Therefore, it is possible that in the Initial Period camelids were killed during prime adult years with an emphasis on non-meat products or people practiced relatively conservative culling practices, perhaps to defend against lean years. Llamas and alpacas at Chiripa may have been more valued for their wool and dung rather than a food resource.

Local trade and lake resources were also highly important for these semi-sedentary horticulturalists. Large quantities of fish scales and bones have been recovered from sites all around the lake basin, and fish remained central to diets for many centuries after plant and animal domestication (Capriles et al. 2008; Capriles et al. 2014; Juengst et al. 2021; Miller et al. 2010; Moore et al. 1999). In addition to the animal resources that the lake provided, totora reeds may have been gathered for consumption and construction of rafts, houses, and other structures (although exactly when and how this plant was used is based largely on ethnographic and ethnohistoric research) (Figure 2.3)

Figure 2.3 Tortora reeds growing in the lake in summer 2012. Photo by author.

22 Life in the Titicaca Basin

(Janusek 2008; Orlove 2002). These horticulturalists also engaged in reciprocal relationships with neighbors in varying ecozones (Janusek 2008). Thus, it seems likely that seasonally migratory, hunting and foraging groups in this region had access to a variety of foods—highland puna and lacustrine resources in addition to goods from lower productive zones. Although these groups were living in semi-permanent villages, fissioning at this time was relatively common, with people easily relocating settlements from time to time, possibly due to a low investment in land resources or seasonal fluctuations in temperature and resources (Bandy 2004; Capriles et al. 2014).

While lake resources continued to be important in the Early Horizon, plant domesticates, especially quinoa and the newly introduced maize, became more common in the lake basin, suggesting that horticultural products increased in importance (Bruno and Whitehead 2003; Stanish 2003; Miller et al. 2021; Murray 2005). Maize in the region may have either been locally grown or traded into the region from lower altitude (Bruno and Whitehead 2003; Chávez and Thompson 2006; Berryman 2010; Logan et al. 2012). The altitude and climate of the Titicaca Basin is at the extreme end of maize's growing range, but modern farmers are able to grow local variants today (Figure 2.4) so it is possible past peoples had similar strategies. Herding domesticated llamas and other camelids was an increasingly important economic strategy in the Early Horizon, making pasture space a more valued commodity (Moore et al. 2007).

Figure 2.4 Lakeside field with maize in spring 2018. Photo by author.

Life in the Titicaca Basin 23

During the Early Horizon, people constructed extensive terraces, remodeling the landscape in a significant way. Terrace walls were as high as three meters and often included additional staircases and access ramps. Undoubtedly, terrace construction was a group project and construction of these walls was very labor intensive. Experimental attempts show that the process of shaping a single stone would have taken at least 40 minutes of labor from four adult men (Chávez, S. 2012). Despite the labor required, these terraces were worth the effort given their agricultural productivity. By constructing large terraces, people prevented soil erosion down the sides of this vertical landscape, increased field space by creating more flat areas, created microclimates suitable to growing crops that require warmer temperatures, and made pasture space for camelids during fallow seasons (Chávez, S. 2012). The construction of terraces and domestication of plants and animals shows a definite increase in landscape investment. This may indicate increased connection or meaning attached to a particular place or the creation of local "temple domains" (Chávez, K. 1997; Chávez and Thompson 2006). These terrace systems have been maintained and occasionally expanded over time, and are still in use today (Figure 2.5).

People began to trade via long-distance trade routes during this time as well, moving goods between regions several hundred

Figure 2.5 Prehispanic terracing and Inka ruins on Isla del Sol (Isla Titicaca). Photo used with permission of Carita Westbook.

kilometers away from the Titicaca Basin. Early Horizon goods from sites around the lake basin are associated with exotic resources, such as obsidian, which were collected at considerable distances from the Titicaca Basin. Obsidian studies at Chiripa showed that the sources of this stone were as far away as Chivay and Alca in the Department of Arequipa in Southern Peru and possibly from as far as Chavin in the Central Peruvian highlands. (Burger et al. 2000). Obsidian flakes have been found in addition to completed tools, indicating that production occurred on site in the lake basin and that the tools did not come into the region accidentally or sporadically (Burger et al. 2000; Stanish et al. 2002). The obsidian for these tools likely came through a "down-the-line" network of communities (Stanish et al. 2002), implying that complicated social networks were involved in moving large quantities of raw material great distances. People may have also been using these trade routes to move less-durable goods such as exotic foodstuffs and coca leaves. Certain foods and ceremonial goods such as coca only grow at lower altitudes. Access to these items would have been reliant on trade networks such as those moving obsidian during the Early Horizon.

The Early Intermediate Period (50 BC–AD 200) (hereafter referred to as the EIP) is marked by an intensification of these processes. Investment in terrestrial resources increased, particularly as the region entered into an extended drought and lake levels dropped (Abbott et al. 1997; Capriles et al. 2014; Juengst et al. 2021). As farming intensified and new social institutions emerged throughout the EIP, Bandy (2004) notes that villages became more stable, with fissioning a less frequent occurrence over time. Investment in and the cost of leaving a settlement became much higher due to reliance on agricultural products and increasingly complex social relationships. Additionally, small agricultural or pastoral fields might now have expanded into once vacant areas, thereby limiting the "open" areas into which people could move (Bruno and Whitehead 2003; Bandy 2004). This trend of decreased settlement fissioning at least demonstrates an increased stress threshold within villages—as conflicts arose, people mediated disagreements rather than split from the community and founded new settlements (Bandy 2004). On the Copacabana Peninsula, archaeological and bioarchaeological studies suggest that groups cooperated to achieve construction and trade tasks, rather than through hierarchy or violent coercion (Chávez, S. 2012; Juengst 2017, 2018).

Occurring along side increasing site stability and terrace construction throughout the Early Horizon and the EIP was the emergence of a previously unknown social institution: a broad scale, regional

Figure 2.6 The reconstructed Yaya-Mama temple Ch'isi, with stone stelae in situ. Photo by author.

religious tradition (Chávez, K. 1988; Chávez, S. 2004; Chávez and Chávez 1976). The Yaya-Mama Religious Tradition is marked by the construction of the sunken temples, carved stone sculptures, the use of supernatural images, and the presence of ritual paraphernalia like ceramic trumpets (Chávez, K. 1988; Chávez, S. 2002; Chávez and Chávez 1970, 1976). Developed at the site of Chiripa during the Initial Period, the religious tradition and its associated sunken temples were present throughout the southern Titicaca Basin by the end of the Early Horizon and continued to be used throughout the EIP (Chávez, K. 1988; Chávez, S. 2004; Stanish 2003). The temples were square or rectangular sunken spaces built on high hills, artificial mounds, or at the foot of towering cliffs (Figure 2.6) (Chávez, S. 2004).

Sculpted stone *stelae* or monoliths, occasionally incorporated into temple walls, were perhaps the most distinctive and important feature of the tradition, in that they were long-lasting and highly visible. These monoliths have been found throughout the lake basin. Carved iconography on these stelae typically included representations of male and female human figures and heads with rayed appendages that may represent supernatural images (Chávez, K. 1988; Chávez, S. 1992, 2002, 2004; Chávez and Chávez 1976; Janusek 2008). The Taraco Yaya-Mama stelae, after which the tradition was named, has become the classic archaeological example of Yaya-Mama iconography: one side of the standing stone sculpture depicted a male figure while the other showed a female. Each character had an elaborate headdress, a checkered belt, and a navel with rays emerging from it, possibly indicating fertility and reproduction. Snakes or serpent-like figures run along the sides between the two figures, representing the Yaya-Mama emphasis on natural images and connections with the earth. Dual complementarity, between male and female, human and nature, life and death, was a recurring theme throughout Yaya-Mama imagery on stelae and special ceramic vessels (Chávez, S. 2002, 2004; Janusek 2008). These themes were repeated in the region for many centuries after Yaya-Mama sites were abandoned, reflecting the enduring power and importance of such images (Burger et al. 2000; Chávez, S. 2004; Cohen 2010).

Ritual paraphernalia, such as ceremonial burners, ceramic trumpets and decorated ceramic vessels of varying size, was another important aspect of the Yaya-Mama tradition (Chávez, K. 1988; Chávez, S. 2004; Janusek 2008). Most ceramics found at Yaya-Mama sites were jars or *ollas* in a range of sizes, bowls, ceremonial burners, or ceramic trumpets. *Ollas* and bowls were often large enough to hold enough food for many people, suggesting feasting, although this varied by site size and location. Fragments of ceramic trumpets were less common than other pieces. Only one trumpet has been reconstructed, from approximately 40 ceramic sherds found scattered across the site and offering structures (Sergio Chávez, personal communication 2010). A few complete trumpets in museum collections have been identified as Yaya-Mama through paste, dimension, and manufacture technique and design. Unfortunately, these pieces lack provenience and context.

Archaeologists disagree on how ritual practice affected the Early Horizon and EIP social roles. While this tradition emerged concurrently with other social changes including increasing sedentism, shifting subsistence practices, and emerging long-distance trade routes, the relationship between religion and other social practices is disputed. Some authors suggest that this emerging ritual tradition represented the development of social hierarchy and status, with new achieved or ascribed elites gathering at these temples and participating in socially valued rituals (Janusek 2008; Stanish 2003). Others suggest that these temples represented an ancestor-focused ritual practice that allowed for local variation between communities but united the lake basin into a common identity (Chávez, S. 2002, 2004; Hastorf 2003; Roddick and Hastorf 2010). Archaeologists have documented the suite of political, social, and economic changes that occurred in the Titicaca Basin during the Early Horizon and EIP, from the import of foreign goods, the increased reliance on domesticated plants and animals, and the emergence of regional ritual. In other parts of the world, developments such as these are often accompanied by social status aggrandizing and emergent social hierarchies (i.e., Earle 1997; Eshed et al. 2010; Larsen 1995). However, given the ecological backdrop for these developments, the situation in the Titicaca Basin may have proceeded differently. How did people living in the lake basin during the Early Horizon navigate these new social institutions and construct their communities? How did people in the southern lake basin build community during the Preceramic, Early Horizon, and Early Intermediate Period throughout large scale social and economic changes? How can studying skeletons provide additional or different insight than the archaeological record?

Burial Sites for this Study

The skeletal sample for this book was excavated from seven archaeological sites on the Copacabana Peninsula: Ch'isi, Cundisa, Muruqullu, Kenasfena, Qhot'a Pata, Qopakati, and Tawa Qeñani (Figure 1.1; Table 2.2). Cundisa and Kenasfena included the earliest burial samples, with first occupation during the Early Horizon (800–50 BC), while the other five sites were occupied during the latter half of the Early Horizon (400–50 BC) throughout the EIP (50 BC–AD 200). Each site and burial sample are described in more detail below, but notably, no habitation sites were associated with these remains—all come from cemetery or ritual contexts. These remains were excavated by the Yaya-Mama Project between 1992 and 2009 with the support of local landowners and community members, many of whom participated throughout the excavation and research process. The skeletons are currently undergoing repatriation to local communities in accordance with original excavation agreements (Chávez, S. 2008a, 2008b).

Ch'isi was a Yaya-Mama temple located on the western portion of the Copacabana Peninsula, located near the modern town of Chissi, and was primarily occupied through the latter half of the Early Horizon and throughout the EIP (i.e., approximately 400 BC–AD 200). The main architectural feature of this site was the sunken temple court and standing stone stelae which featured a rayed head (Figure 2.6). Surrounding the court were rings of burials, in tombs lined with stone.

Table 2.2 Burial sample contributions from each site

Site	Ch'isi	Cundisa	Muruqullu	Kenasfena	Qopakati	Tawa Qeñani	Qhot'a Pata	Total
Number of Preceramic Individuals	0	0	14	0	0	0	0	14
Number of Early Horizon Individuals	5	2	37	2	0	0	0	46
Number of Early Intermediate Period Individuals	47	31	0	0	7	6	2	93
Total	52	33	51	2	7	6	2	153

These burials were oriented roughly parallel to the sunken court walls, with four individuals placed at each corner and turned 45 degrees (Chávez, S. 2004). Most tombs included one individual, although a few contained remains of several individuals. Some tombs had been reopened occasionally, either to add more individuals or potentially leave offerings of food and drink. Few tombs had associated grave goods beyond simple and often broken ceramics (Sergio Chávez personal communication 2012). A total of 52 EIP individuals were interred at this site.

Cundisa was located in the center of what is now modern Copacabana, and has evidence of continuous occupation and use from the Early Horizon through modern day (Chávez, S. 2008a). This site is currently beneath the modern governmental office of Copacabana. Burials were excavated in 1993 and 2009 from strata associated with the Early Horizon and EIP. These burials had worse preservation than burials at other sites, likely because they were not buried in the same stone-lined tombs noted elsewhere but in earthen pits (Chávez, S. 2008a). These burials included some utilitarian pottery but fewer ritual items than burials at other sites (Stanislava Chávez personal communication 2012). The Cundisa sample included at least 33 individuals.

Muruqullu was located on the northern part of the peninsula, near the modern town of Sampaya (Figure 2.7), and had several stages of occupation. People were first buried at Muruqullu during the Terminal Preceramic (3000–1500 BC), in pits dug directly into the bedrock and associated with lithic material used for deer and camelid hunting (Juengst et al. 2017a). Fourteen Preceramic individuals were excavated from this Preceramic cemetery. Subsequently, people built a Yaya-Mama temple at this location, used at the end of the Early Horizon (i.e., approximately 400–50 BC). During the Yaya-Mama occupation, people used the site for burial. There were three burials around the temple, diagonally placed at corners, as seen at Ch'isi, but the majority of the burials were in the cemetery-like area next to the temple (Sergio Chávez personal communication 2012). Early Horizon burials were identified by the inclusion of Yaya-Mama pottery, stone tools, or by having stone-lined tombs. Grave goods were not elaborate but usually utilitarian pottery associated with serving food and drink (Sergio Chávez and Stanislava Chávez, personal communication 2012). Thirty-seven individuals were associated with the Yaya-Mama temple occupation of the site.

Kenasfena is a Yaya-Mama temple on the southeastern portion of the Copacabana Peninsula, near the modern town of Huayllani close

Figure 2.7 The modern church at Sampaya, near the location of Muruqullu. Photo by author.

to the Straits of Tiquina. Survey and limited excavation demonstrated the presence of standing stone stelae (Figure 2.8) and at least three temple construction events during the Early Horizon (800–50 BC). Test excavations also revealed two burials, each containing one individual and fragmentary ritual pottery (Sergio Chávez personal communication 2012).

Qhot'a Pata is located in the valley adjacent to and contemporaneous with the temple at Ch'isi. Identified by a collection of EIP pottery, stone tools, and two human burials, the use of this site was unclear. Both individuals from Qhot'a Pata were buried in individual earthen pits (Sergio Chávez personal communication 2012).

Qopakati is a Yaya-Mama temple located on the southwestern portion of the Copacabana Peninsula, close to the modern border between Peru and Bolivia. This site was also associated with early rock art, carvings, and paintings of camelids and an Andean cross. This art may have been contemporaneous with or postdated the EIP temple. Qopakati excavations only included preliminary test pits and a trench, so less is known about temple structure and orientation. However,

Figure 2.8 Standing stone stelae at Kenasfena. Photo by author.

the trench uncovered several burials associated with the temple that appeared to have stone-lined graves. Most of these burials contained the remains of one or two individuals, totaling seven individuals (Sergio Chávez personal communication 2012).

Tawa Qeñani is a small site on the eastern portion of the Copacabana Peninsula, just south of and contemporaneous with Ch'isi. Limited excavation was performed at this site, but test pits revealed several burials associated with ritual pottery and Yaya-Mama-style tombs (Sergio Chávez personal communication 2012). Interestingly, all six of the EIP burials at Tawa Qeñani included juvenile individuals.

The Burial Sample

In total, there were 153 individuals excavated from Preceramic, Early Horizon, and EIP contexts on the Copacabana Peninsula (Table 2.2). Fourteen of these individuals dated to the Preceramic Period, 46 to the Early Horizon, and 93 to the Early Intermediate Period. Importantly, this sample includes individuals from a variety of demographic groups, including adults and non-adults, and adults presenting male, female, and indeterminate sex characteristics. This is important as it demonstrates that although the burials come from special sites (i.e., places associated with predominantly ritual rather than domestic contexts), a wide range of individuals was able to access them.

Age-at-Death of the Burial Sample

Age-at-death can be estimated from various skeletal features, including dental eruption and wear, long bone growth and fusion, changes to the form and appearance of parts of the pelvis, and fusion of the cranial sutures. Tooth eruption and wear were used as the primary indicators of age when dentition was available for the individual. Tooth eruption and tooth root formation were scored using the standard eruption chart (Ubelaker 1989), paying special attention to the eruption of the adult first, second, and third molars, erupting at approximately 6, 12, and 18–22 years, respectively. Additionally, dental wear was based on scoring systems developed by Murphy (1959) and Smith (1984) and diagram widely used for age estimation (Buikstra and Ubelaker 1994). Dental wear is not a perfect system of age estimation because attrition may be caused by factors other than time, including amount of grit in the diet and occupational uses of teeth. However, by combining this method with the skeletal methods listed below, dental wear may help narrow age ranges for older adults.

When teeth were not available, age estimation was based on the appearance of the pubic symphysis, fusion of the epiphyses of long bones, and cranial suture closure. The pubic symphysis, located on the front portion of the pelvis, undergoes a series of standard changes throughout the life course. Intact pubic symphyses were compared to the Todd (Todd 1921a, 1921b) and Suchey-Brooks (Brooks and Suchey 1990; Suchey and Katz 1986) pubic symphysis mold series and subsequently gave them the corresponding score and age category. The ends of long bones fuse throughout childhood and adolescence. This pattern of fusion is notably regular across populations, within a certain range, and can be used to estimate approximate age for young individuals. Notable epiphyses were the proximal and distal tibia (fusing around 12–16 years), the distal femur (14–16 years), the iliac crest (17–20 years), and the medial clavicle (20–25 years), as these unions mark the upper limits of childhood and adolescence, often an important social moment in one's life (Buikstra and Ubelaker 1994; Halcrow and Tayles 2011; Lewis 2007; Sofaer 2006; Ubelaker 1989). Finally, the sutures of the cranium slowly fuse over one's lifetime; they

Table 2.3 Age estimates for the burial sample

Period	Infant	Juvenile (3–12)	Adolescent (13–17)	Young Adult (18–25)	Adult 25+	Total
PC	0	2	0	4	8	14
EH	6	9	5	3	23	46
EIP	10	27	3	19	34	93
Total	16	38	8	26	65	153

are open at birth, remain relatively open throughout childhood, and undergo fusion through middle and old adulthood. They are typically fully obliterated by 55 years of age. When articulated crania were present, suture patterns were compared to a standard set of images of progressive suture closure (Meindl and Lovejoy 1985; photos by P. Walker in Buikstra and Ubelaker 1994).

The age categories include adult (over 25 years of age), young adult (18–25 years), adolescent (13–17 years), juvenile (3–12 years), and infant (birth–2 years). When an age range could not be estimated or groups were lumped for analysis, I used adult (18 years and older) and non-adult (under 18 years). These age categories were selected because they represent moments of significant biological change over the life course which often have social consequences. Biological processes like weaning and puberty are often cross-culturally important to social status, as they reflect new periods of independence, new identities, and a significant shift in relationships between people (Halcrow and Tayles 2011:336; Lewis 2007; Sofaer 2011).

Overall, there were 91 adults and 62 non-adults in the sample overall (Table 2.3). Among the Preceramic burials, there were 8 adults, 4 young adults and 2 juveniles. The Early Horizon burials included 23 adults, 3 young adults, 5 adolescents, 9 juveniles, and 6 infants. The EIP burials included 65 adults, 26 young adults, 8 adolescents, 38 juveniles, and 16 infants. The EIP sample does include significantly more young adults and juveniles than the Early Horizon sample (χ^2 (1, n=137) = 9.90, p=0.042, where p< 0.05 is significant). This indicates some change in mortality, fertility, and/or burial selection between the time periods and will be discussed more in Chapters 3 and 4.

Sex Estimation of the Burial Sample

As a species, humans tend towards sexual dimorphism, based on chromosomes, hormones, and anatomy. However, the biological assessment of these traits into two discrete sexes is a practice stemming from relatively recent European-based medicine and science; yet, dichomotous sex in lived bodies is not as straightforward and it is often the search for two sexes that create these categories (Gellar 2009, 2017; Joyce 2017). The osteological assessment of skeletons for sex-linked traits is therefore somewhat fraught, and should be done with reflexivity and awareness of the researcher's own biases (Walrath 2017). Despite these potential biases, sex and gender are sometimes linked and may hold important information about social roles for past and present peoples. Understanding how sex and/or gender impacted people's experiences of power is thus critical for assessing social inequality. In this book, sex is not equated with gender but considered as one line of evidence towards understanding embodied power in the past.

Sex was estimated for all adolescent, young adult, and adult individuals when pelvic and cranial remains were present. Pelvic remains were privileged during sex estimation, as these bones are most affected by sex-linked hormones and reproductive needs and consequences. Female pelves tend to be wider overall and marked by the presence and appearance of the following features: the subpubic concavity, the ischiopubic ramus, the ventral arc, the greater sciatic notch, the pelvic outlet, and the preauricular sulcus. These features were scored following methods developed by Buikstra and Meilke (1985), and Phenice (1969). Definitive sex categories (female, male) were only assigned to those with well-preserved pelvic characteristics. Individuals with ambiguous pelvic traits but suggestive cranial traits were assigned probable sex categories (probable female, probable male) according to standards in Buikstra and Ubelaker (1994) following methods developed by Acsadi and Nemeskeri (1970). Sex was not estimated for individuals without crania or pelves or for those under 15 years of age. For statistical analyses, probable and definite sex categories were combined (i.e., combining probable females and females) but in qualitative observations, these were maintained as separate categories.

Overall, there were 8 individuals estimated to be female, 15 probable female, 29 probable male, 13 male, and 88 individuals of indeterminate sex (Table 2.4). Among the Preceramic burials, there were 2 individuals estimated to be female, 6 estimated to be male, 1 estimated as probable male, and 5 individuals of indeterminate sex. The Early Horizon burials included 1 individual estimated to be female, 6 probable female, 13 probable male, 2 male, and 24 of indeterminate sex. The EIP burials included 5 individuals estimated to be females, 9

Table 2.4 Estimated sex of individuals in burial sample

Period	Female	Probable Female	Indeterminate	Probable Male	Male	Total
PC	2	0	5	1	6	14
EH	1	6	24	13	2	46
EIP	5	9	59	15	5	93
Total	8	15	88	29	13	153

probable female, 15 probable male, 5 male, and 59 individuals of indeterminate sex. There are not significant differences in estimated sex between the burial samples.

This burial sample represents people who lived during three different periods in Copacabana history, practicing different types of subsistence, living in varied settlements, and engaging in new religious practices. While the sample certainly does not include everyone who lived in the peninsula during these periods, these individuals provide a glimpse into the diverse experiences people may have had. Assessing these skeletons for skeletal lesions of stress, labor, and malnutrition, markers of relatedness and biological distance, strontium and dietary isotopes, trauma, and indicators of cultural modification provides insight into the questions about power on the Copacabana Peninsula of Bolivia during the Preceramic, Early Horizon, and Early Intermediate Period.

3 Daily Living
Sustenance, Stress, and Strain

Power and social relationships are embedded in daily practice through what we eat, and how we experience health and disease. This chapter explores how skeletal indicators of stress from malnutrition and disease, skeletal indicators of physical labor, and isotopic indicators of dietary trends changed for Titicaca Basin peoples. Combining analyses of skeletal manifestations of stress and isotopic studies of diet provides a more complete picture of access to food for past peoples. In the lake basin during the Preceramic, Early Horizon, and Early Intermediate Period, there were significant changes in food, as people domesticated animals and increasingly relied on agricultural plants. However, it is possible that these dietary shifts elevated risk of malnutrition for everyone, or that not everyone had equal access to adequate resources. It is also possible that as food production strategies changed, labor fell more heavily on the shoulders of some. Foods seen as special may have been restricted to certain individuals or groups and not shared more broadly. The skeletal and isotopic records thus provide valuable insight into these processes.

Skeletal Lesions of Malnutrition, Stress, and Disease

Malnutrition and stress affect skeletons in a few important ways. In general, these lesions are nonspecific, meaning they cannot be linked to one particular cause but broadly reflect conditions that caused physiological stress for the body. They represent times when the body protected itself from an intruding pathogen, reacted to a micronutrient deficiency, and stopped growth and development to conserve resources.

Periosteal reactions are caused by changes to the outer layer of bone and appear as areas of abnormal porosity, new bone formation, and added bone on top of the smooth bony surface (Aufderheide et al.

2018; DeWitte 2014; Ortner 2003). While periosteal reactions can stem from many causes, their presence is generally tied to systemic infections when lesions are found throughout the skeleton. Healing of these lesions can indicate the ability of the person to recover from a stressful event (DeWitte 2014; Ortner 2003). Interestingly, because these lesions are chronic, individuals with periosteal lesions may be more resilient than those without, given that they survived the stressor long enough to allow these lesions to form (Wood et al. 1992). However, periosteal lesions are positively correlated with increased mortality (DeWitte 2014), showing that while individuals may initially be resilient, the chronic stress associated with these lesions erodes individuals' bodily and immune capability to respond to insults over time.

Osteomyelitis occurs when a bacterial infection enters the marrow cavity of long bones, causing inflammation and new bony growth along the interior of the bones. These infections typically form a draining sinus and are often accompanied by exterior periosteal reactions as well (Roberts and Manchester 2007). Relative healing, or lack thereof, can indicate the ability of the person to recover from these stress events, providing a commentary on overall individual health.

Cribra orbitalia (CO) and porotic hyperostosis (PH) are porous lesions in the eye orbits and on the cranium, respectively, and can co-occur or occur independently of one another (Oxenham and Cavill 2010; Stuart-Macadam 1985, 1992). They generally indicate stressful episodes in childhood, stemming from insufficient nutrient intake, disease episodes, and/or high levels of bodily parasites (Blom et al. 2005; Goodman and Rose 1990; Kent 1986; Stuart-Macadam 1985, 1992; Walker et al. 2009). CO and PH have been linked to a variety of nutrient deficiencies such as iron, scurvy, vitamin B12, and folic acid, and probably often result from several nutrient deficiencies co-occurring, since these types of malnutrition often go together (Brickley and Ives 2006; Klaus 2012; McIlvaine 2015; Rothschild 2002; Walker 1986; Walker et al. 2009). Evidence for healing of the cranial lesions gives some indication of whether the stresses were relieved.

Linear enamel hypoplasia (LEH) are defects that occur in dental enamel, due to episodes of extreme nutritional or immune stress during childhood. LEH represent a break in the creation of dental enamel during tooth formation, as the body devotes resources to immune protection or bodily maintenance while under duress. They form upon recovery from a stressful episode, once a tooth is able to start creating more dental enamel (Armelagos et al. 2009). The presence of LEH therefore indicates survivorship of a childhood stressful event, although the entry of the person into the skeletal record may represent succumbing to a later episode (Wilson 2014).

Skeletal Indicators of Physical Labor and Repetitive Tasks

Daily tasks that require repetitive labor can become embodied as bones and joints respond to the biomechanical forces placed upon them (Becker 2020; Jurmain et al. 2011). This takes the form of changes to the shape of long bones, alterations to the places where muscles attach to bones, and degeneration of joint surfaces. These processes are cumulative and dependent on many variables, such as age, sex, and genetics, making them a common occurrence for adult humans and generally unreliable for reconstructing *particular* activities (despite the best efforts of many bioarchaeologists) (Jurmain 2013, Jurmain et al. 2011); however, by assessing patterns of these markers across a population and with contextual control, it is possible to see trends in overall bodily stress (Ortner 2011). In particular, tasks and everyday practices contribute to the distribution and severity of degenerative joint disease (Becker 2020; Larsen 1995; Jurmain 2013; Roberts and Manchester 2007; Schrader 2019).

Osteoarthritis (OA) is the most common of degenerative joint diseases among living and past peoples. OA is complex, multifactorial condition generally defined as a disorder involving a buildup of bone surrounding skeletal joints and margins associated with loss of synovial cartilage on joint surfaces (Larsen 1995; Jurmain 2013; Waldron 2019) This condition can stem from a variety of causes, including age, genetics, weight, hormones, skeletal trauma, and repetitive labor. Primary OA results from mechanical stress in the absence of a traumatic injury or other underlying cause to prompt the abnormal bone growth, whereas secondary OA stems from genetic predispositions (such as rheumatoid arthritis) or skeletal trauma and dislocation. While differentiating between the two can at times be difficult, primary OA is often associated with repetitive motions or regular load-bearing and is thus useful for assessing behavior and labor patterns in the past (Larsen 1995, 2015; Schrader 2019; Zhang et al. 2017).

The appearance of OA on skeletons can take the form of porosity, lipping, or eburnation, or a combination of the three. Abnormal porosity and lipping can result from osteolytic and osteophytic activity: the erosion and subsequent creation of new bone in response to strain (Felson et al. 2000; Waldron 2019). Eburnation is caused by two bones coming into direct contact once protective cartilage has been worn away and is correlated with highly repetitive motions. This condition may appear as a polished or even shiny area of the joint surface as the bones repeatedly come into contact (Buikstra and Ubelaker 1994; Jurmain 2013; Schrader 2019). When these conditions appear together, bioarchaeologists usually assess the joint has having been affected by OA (Larsen 2015; Rogers and Waldron 1995).

Osteoarthritis is also linked with load-bearing and vertebral conditions such as porosity of the vertebral bodies, osteophytosis, spondylosis, and Schmorl's nodes (Ortner 2003; Jurmain et al. 2011). Extra bony growth in the vertebral column ranges from lipping on vertebral bodies and articular facets through complete fusion of one or more vertebra (Buikstra and Ubelaker 1994; Larsen 2015). Spondylosis and Schmorl's nodes are fractures and depressions in the bodies of vertebra (Junghanns and Schmorl 1971). Like other types of OA, vertebral conditions are caused by a number of factors, including bipedalism (Bridges 1994), load-bearing (Junghanns and Schmorl 1971; Zhang et al. 2017), occupation and activity (Becker 2017; Larsen 1995; Zhang et al. 2017; Schrader 2019) and trauma (Zhang et al. 2017).

By assessing OA across a population at multiple joint surfaces, it is possible to reconstruct overall patterns of labor. While specific activities are likely not identifiable, repetitive motions and overall stress to the body may be observed through carefully collected evidence, contextualized interpretations, and population-level observations (Becker 2020; Larsen 2015; Pearson and Buikstra 2006; Schrader 2019). Changes to the frequency of OA may indicate shifts in labor patterns, and the clustering of OA on certain individuals in connection with other skeletal lesions might suggest heavier workloads.

Investigations of Diet Based on Stable Isotope Analyses

Many foods have distinct ratios of the stable isotopes of carbon ($^{13}C/^{12}C$) and nitrogen ($^{15}N/^{14}N$), and when eaten, these ratios are incorporated into human skeletons and dentition. Carbon isotopes generally reflect certain types of plant foods consumed, while nitrogen isotopes are linked to protein consumption and trophic level (Ambrose 1993; Schoeninger and Moore 1992). While these isotopes cannot reflect specific meals, they can show us what types of foods were consumed on average during a person's childhood (from teeth) and later in life (from bones). A combination of tooth and bone samples can show changes within a person's lifetime (i.e., if their diet changed between childhood and adulthood) and more broadly within a community (i.e., if children typically ate different diets than adults). A mix of tooth and bone samples were selected from the Copacabana individuals in order to capture this variation, discussed more below.

Carbon isotopes ($^{13}C/^{12}C$) vary based on the type of photosynthetic pathway a plant uses to absorb energy. C_3 plants do not absorb the heavier isotope (^{13}C) during photosynthesis and thus have negative stable isotope ratios, averaging −26.5‰. These types of plants generally include temperate trees and shrubs and high-altitude grasses. Comparatively, C_4 plants are less discriminatory towards $_{13}C$ and have less negative ratios, averaging around −12.5‰. C_4 plants include tropical grasses; in South America, maize and amaranths are the most commonly consumed C_4 plants. CAM (Crassulacean Acid Metabolism) plants, such as pineapple and cacti, can shift between C_3 and C_4 pathways, which gives them an intermediate isotopic signature (Smith and Epstein 1971; Troughton et al. 1974).

Nitrogen isotopes ($^{15}N/^{14}N$) vary based on environment and trophic level in marine and terrestrial environments. Some plants obtain nitrogen directly from the atmosphere, giving them a 0‰ nitrogen signature, while most other plants absorb enriched nitrogen from the soil. This enriched nitrogen accumulates by 2–6‰ per trophic level, as plants, prey, and predators are successively consumed (O'Connell et al. 2012; Schoeninger and DeNiro 1984).

Carbon and nitrogen isotopes are incorporated into skeletal material in a few ways. Carbon in bone mineral apatite carbonate ($\delta^{13}C_{ca}$) accurately reflects the whole diet (proteins, fats, and carbohydrates) while the carbon in bone collagen ($\delta^{13}C_{co}$) reflects mostly dietary protein. Using this knowledge, researchers have created predictive models and comparative schema to demonstrate diets with varying proportions of C_3/C_4 foods and nitrogen sources, highlighting diets of entirely terrestrial sources, entirely marine sources, and a range of variation between the two (Ambrose and Norr 1993; Froehle et al. 2012; Kellner and Schoeninger 2007). Of particular use for this book is a multivariate diet reconstruction model that incorporates $\delta^{13}C_{ca}$, $\delta^{13}C_{co}$, and $\delta^{15}N$ (Froehle et al. 2012). Using archaeological human data and models, they model five "centroids": (1): 100% C_3 diet/protein, (2): 30:70 C_3:C_4 diet, >50% C_4 protein, (3): 50:50 C_3:C_4 diet, marine protein, (4): 70:30 C_3:C_4 diet, >65% C_3 protein, and (5): 30:70 C_3:C_4 diet, >65% C_3 protein.

Stress, Labor, and Diet during the Preceramic Period

During the Preceramic, 58% (7/12) of individuals displayed some type of skeletal lesion associated with stress and malnutrition (Table 3.1;

Table 3.1 Skeletal lesions of stress and disease by time period

	Periosteal Rx	Osteomyelitis	CO	PH	LEH	Total
PC	4/11 (36%)	1/11 (9%)	1/5 (20%)	1/6 (17%)	1/10 (10%)	7/12 (58%)
Adult F/PF	1	0	0	0	0	1/2
Adult M/PM	2	0	1	1	0	4/6
Adult I	1	1	0	0	0	1/2
Juvenile	0	0	0	0	1	1/2
EH	13/35 (37%)	1/35 (3%)	8/20 (40%)	7/35 (20%)	9/37 (24%)	26/40 (65%)
Adult F/PF	3	1	2	2	0	4/8
Adult M/PM	6	0	1	1	2	8/15
Adult I	1	0	0	1	0	1/4
Juvenile	3	0	5	3	7	13/18
EIP	20/61 (33%)	4/61 (7%)	18/34 (53%)	10/50 (20%)	9/73 (12%)	40/70 (57%)
Adult F/PF	6	1	2	1	1	9/10*
Adult M/PM	8	3	5	4	0	13/20
Adult I	4	0	2	0	1	6/16
Juvenile	2	0	9	5	7	14/24

*EIP Adult F/PF = X^2 (3, N = 70) = 10.1772, p = .017119
(PC = Preceramic, EH = Early Horizon, EIP = Early Intermediate Period)
Note: Starred results are statistically significant outliers.

42 Daily Living: Sustenance, Stress, and Strain

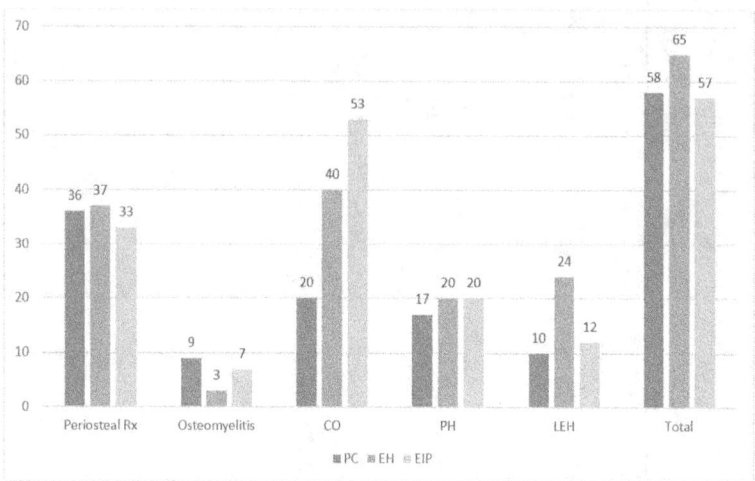

Figure 3.1 Percent of burial samples displaying pathological lesions from each time period.

Figures 3.1, 3.2). The most common skeletal lesions were periosteal reactions, observable on four of 11 individuals (Figure 3.2a). One of these individuals experienced osteomyelitis alongside periosteal reactions indicating severe infection (Figure 3.2b), while another two individuals had cranial porosities associated with nutritional deficiencies (Figure 3.2c). The majority of these individuals (4/6) were male or probable male adults, while one female adult and one adult of indeterminate sex also experienced these lesions. One juvenile individual had a single LEH on each mandibular canine.

Evidence of degenerative joint disease and osteoarthritis was present on 9 (81%) of 11 observable individuals (Table 3.2; Figures 3.3, 3.4). Only the two juvenile individuals did not present osteoarthritis of any kind, consistent with the expected increases of OA with age. This included lipping on the shoulder and elbow joints of 9 of 11 observable individuals (Figure 3.4d), lipping on the hip and knee joints of 6 of 11 observable individuals, and eburnation on the knee of one individual. This rate of hip and knee degeneration is statistically significantly higher than later periods (χ^2 (3, N = 73) = 8.7175, p = .01779). Vertebral lipping and pitting were also fairly common, particularly in the cervical and lumbar vertebrae, and was observed on eight of ten observable vertebral columns (Figure 3.4a, 3.4b). Four individuals had

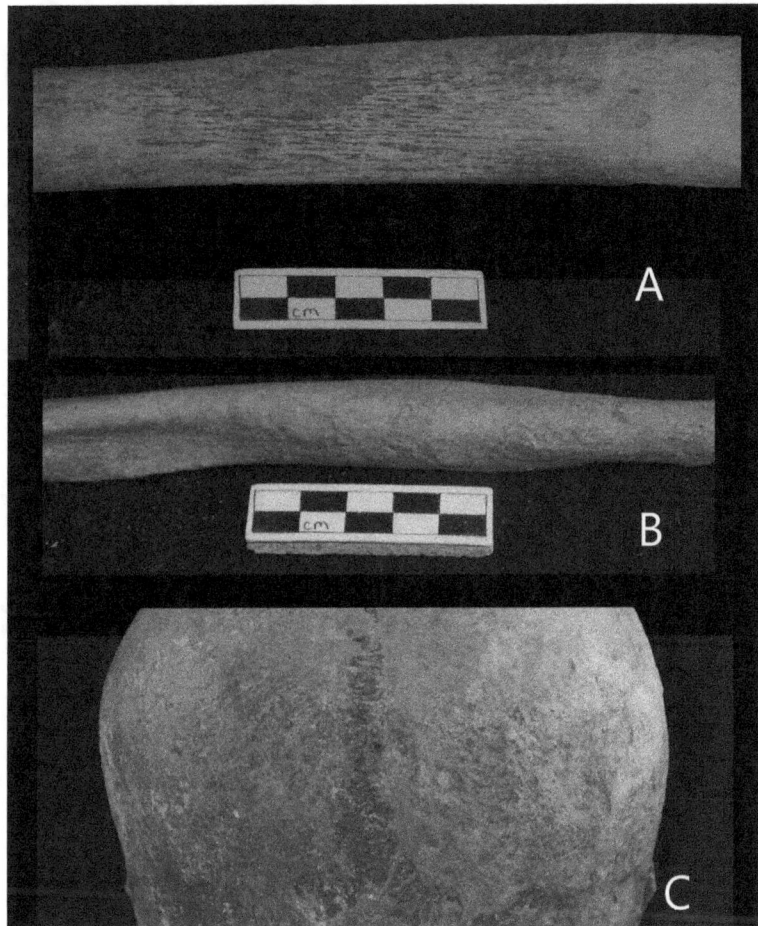

Figure 3.2 Examples of pathological lesions from the Preceramic burials, including periosteal reactions on a tibia (A), osteomyelitis of a fibula (note the swollen and uneven appearance of the exterior surface) (B), and pitting on the posterior of a skull (C).

Schmorl's nodes and compression of the lumbar vertebrae (Figure 3.4c). While rates of OA were high, the proliferative lipping was usually slight and only one young adult individuals suffered from multiple affected joints and more extreme vertebral conditions. Rates of OA did not vary statistically by estimated sex category.

Daily Living: Sustenance, Stress, and Strain

Table 3.2 Frequency of osteoarthritis at various joint surfaces

Period	Age-at-Death of Affected	Shoulder and Elbow OA	Hip and Knee OA	Vertebral Degeneration
Preceramic	Total	9/11 (81%)	6/11 (54%)*	8/10 (80%)
	20–30 years	4/6 (66%)	2/6 (33%)	4/5 (80%)
	30+ years	5/5 (100%)	4/5 (80%)	4/5 (80%)
Early Horizon	Total	15/24 (63%)	2/24 (8%)	15/21 (71%)
	12–20 years	0/5	0/5	2/5 (40%)
	20–30 years	10/12 (83%)	1/13 (8%)	9/12 (55%)
	30+ years	5/7 (71%)	1/6 (17%)	4/4 (100%)
EIP	Total	21/35 (60%)	11/38 (29%)	18/29 (62%)
	12–20 years	0/2	0/3	0/1
	20–30 years	16/25 (64%)	7/25 (28%)	13/20 (65%)
	30+ years	5/7 (71%)	4/10 (40%)	5/8 (63%)

Note: Significant results are starred.

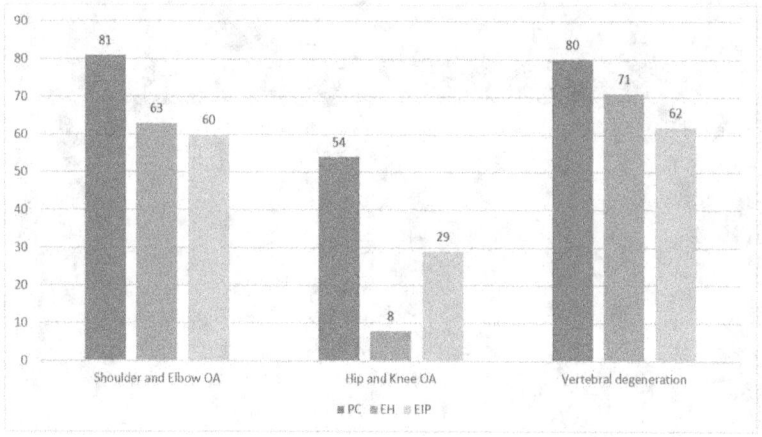

Figure 3.3 Percent of burial samples displaying osteoarthritic from each time period.

Preceramic foragers have high nitrogen signatures, low carbon collagen values, and carbon spacing that implies a mixed C_3-C_4, lacustrine and terrestrial diet (Table 3.3; Figures 3.5, 3.6). This is consistent with (bio)archaeological evidence for their hunting wild game and collecting wild lake resources (Juengst et al. 2017a). Their low carbon collagen values (statistically different from other time periods, according to a Kruskal-Wallis statistical test ($\chi 2 (5) = 15.839$, $p=.007$), reflects

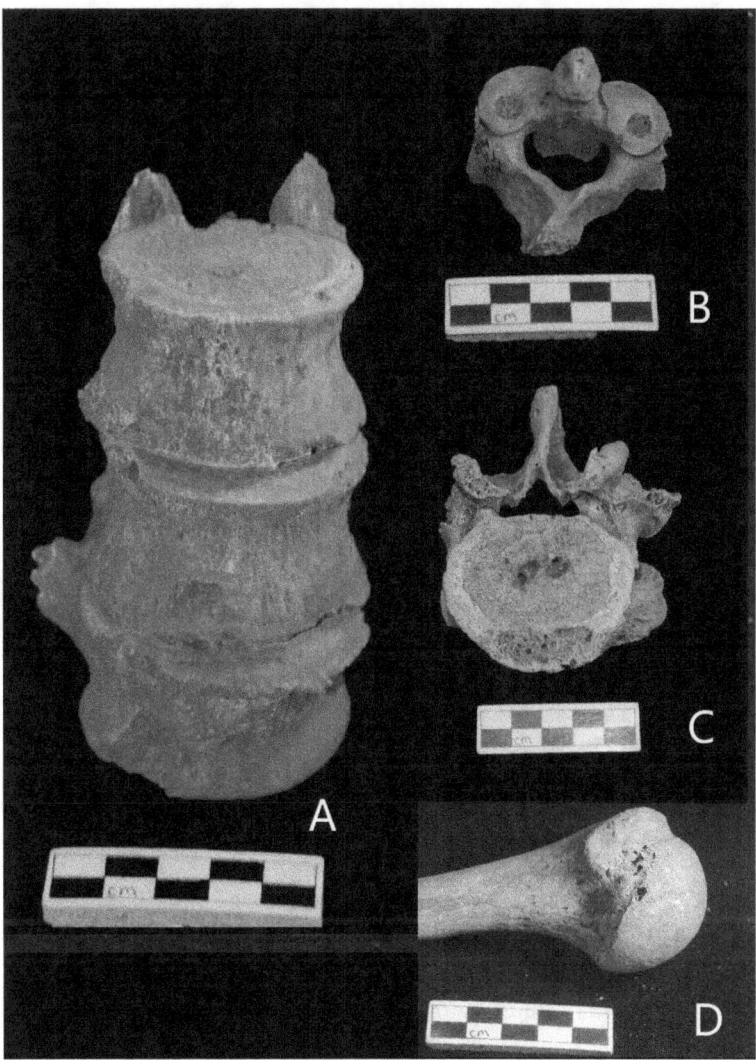

Figure 3.4 Examples of osteoarthritis from the Preceramic burials, including lipping on the edges of lumbar vertebral bodies (A), pitting on the superior articular facets of the 2nd cervical vertebra (B), a Schmorl's node on the body of a lumbar vertebra (C), and pitting and lipping on the margin of a humeral head (D).

46 Daily Living: Sustenance, Stress, and Strain

Table 3.3 Mean isotope values by time period

Period	Total Average $\delta^{15}N_{co}$	Total Average $\delta^{13}C_{ca\text{-}co}$	Total Average $\delta^{13}C_{ap}$	Total Average $\delta^{13}C_{co}$
PC	11.54	5.26	−11.50	−16.64*
EH	10.37	5.73	−12.65	−18.32
EIP	8.77*	6.44	−12.34	−18.77

(PC = Preceramic, EH = Early Horizon, EIP = Early Intermediate Period)
Preceramic individuals were outliers for carbon collagen values according to a Kruskal-Wallis statistical test ($\chi 2$ (5) = 15.839, p = .007).
Note: Starred averages are statistically significant outliers.

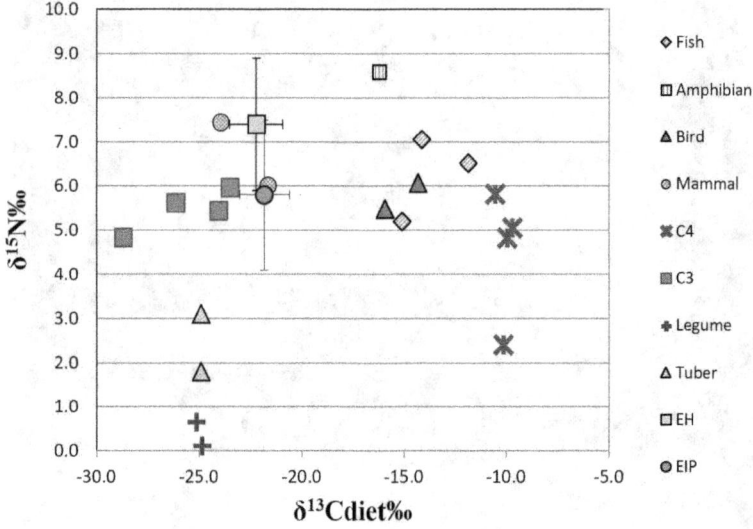

Figure 3.5 Dietary isotopic results. Modern plant and animal samples with human mean values by time period. Human mean error bars are one standard deviation. (PC = Preceramic, EH = Early Horizon, EIP = Early Intermediate Period).

consumption of C_4-rich protein. In comparison with Froehle et al.'s centroids, these foragers consume more C_4 resources than predicted for Centroid 4 (70:30 C_3:C_4 diet, >65% C_3 protein) (Figure 3.6).

Combining these lines of evidence (skeletal lesions, osteoarthritis, and isotopes), it seems that Preceramic peoples worked hard and were relatively well-nourished, likely due to the reliance on ample lake resources during a wet time in the Titicaca Basin (Abbot

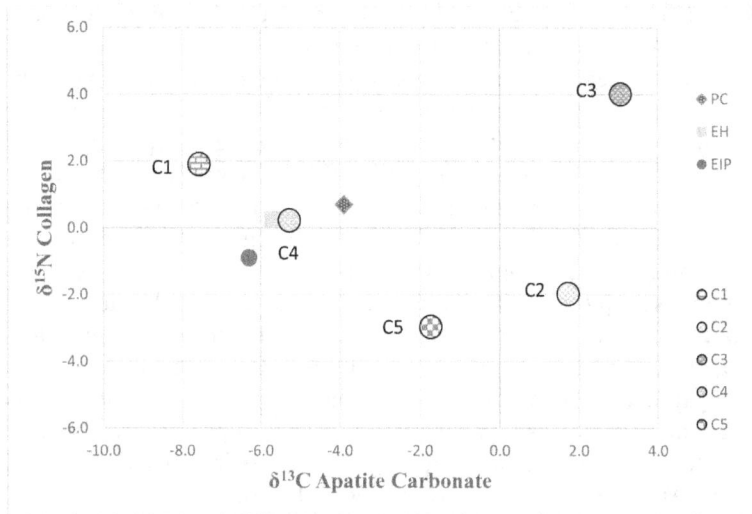

Figure 3.6 Distribution of average $\delta^{13}C$ apatite carbonate values for each time period compared to K-means cluster centroids for dietary estimation developed by Froehle et al. (2012). (PC = Preceramic, EH = Early Horizon, EIP = Early Intermediate Period; C1-C5 indicate the five clusters from Froehle et al. 2012).

et al. 1997; Juengst et al. 2021). Archaeological animal remains indicate that Preceramic peoples likely had some domesticated animals (llamas and alpacas) (Capriles et al. 2014). Isotopically, these individuals demonstrate high protein consumption, which could have stemmed from eating these new domesticates, or from hunting and fishing. Interestingly, they also have the lowest carbon collagen values, which disproportionately represents carbon in the protein portion of diet (Lee-Thorp et al. 1989; Juengst et al. 2021). This implies that the sources of protein for Preceramic peoples consumed more C_4 resources than protein sources in other time periods.

Notably, Miller et al. (2010) report a uniquely wide range of isotopic signatures for modern aquatic plants (and fish feeding on those plants) from Lake Wiñaymarka. In fact, some water plants and algae are more ^{13}C-enriched than maize and amaranths, and fish feeding on these plants are likewise enriched. Conversely, wild highland camelids tend to have more depleted carbon signatures, as compared with later domesticated camelids foddered on maize or marine algae (Finucane et al. 2006; Szpak et al. 2014). Thus, while Preceramic foragers were likely hunting wild terrestrial mammals in addition to fishing, it seems likely that domesticated camelids did not feature regularly in diets, or were already being foddered with lake resources.

Early experiences with infectious disease and bodily stress may have been an issue for Preceramic peoples, as four adult individuals and one juvenile exhibited lesions associated with pathogens and almost all adults suffered some sort of osteoarthritis. While we cannot know the exact cause of the pathological lesions, it is possible that increased contact with domesticated animals led to disease transfer. Moore et al. (2007) suggest that people may have collected camelid dung for fuel, as wood is scarce at the high altitude of the lake basin. While a useful resource, dung collecting would also facilitate the transfer of intestinal parasites and bacteria from animal to human. Other parasites or infectious pathogens could have been stemmed from eating fish as well, as indigenous Titicaca fish do carry several types of parasite and aquatic parasites have been archaeologically documents in other parts of the Andes (Araújo et al. 2011; Patrucco et al. 1983).

Elbow osteoarthritis is commonly identified in archaeological skeletons, and is a useful indictor of motion and use as the elbow joint is less impacted by osteoarthritis linked to age (Bridges 1992). The high frequency of elbow osteoarthritis may indicate regular flexion/extension of the arm, perhaps associated with daily activities such as preparing hides, hunting, and food preparation. Other Andean forager-herders generally demonstrated similar rates of osteoarthritis than seen here (Shults 2020), although coastal forager-fishers often demonstrated less than their inland contemporaries (Ponce 2010; Rhode 2006; Titelbaum 2012). Perhaps the more vertical landscape of the lake basin elevated the strain on the lower body, as people moved throughout their environment.

However, lesions associated with disease and trauma showed evidence of healing and the osteoarthritis present does not seem to have limited their movement or ability to acquire resources, demonstrating the capability of these people to recover from bodily insults and take care for each other. Additionally, while disease may have been an issue, nutrition seems to have been adequate for most Preceramic peoples. Only one adult male had cranial lesions associated with malnutrition. This is not surprising, as Preceramic peoples were fairly mobile and could access diverse resources should one or more fail.

Stress, Labor, and Diet during the Early Horizon

During the Early Horizon, 65% (26/40) of individuals experienced some sort of bodily insult, as reflected by skeletal indicators of stress

Daily Living: Sustenance, Stress, and Strain   49

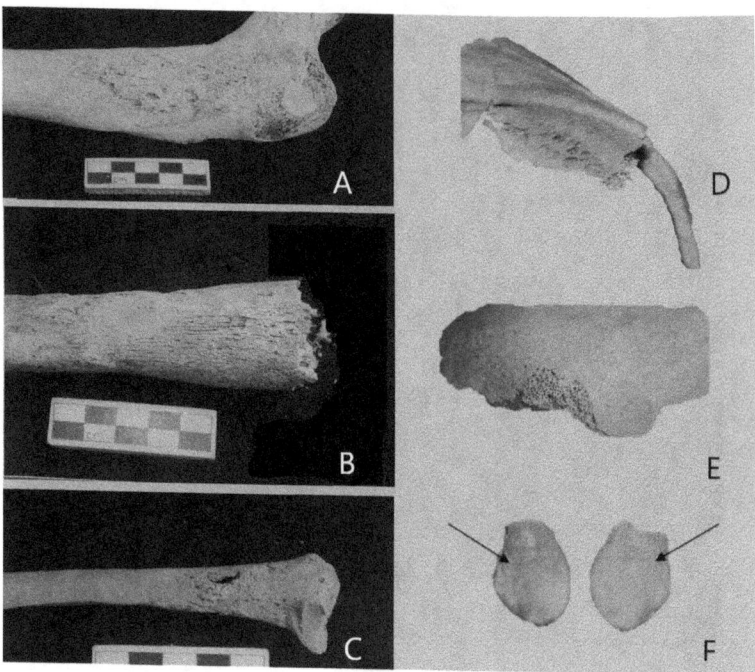

Figure 3.7 Examples of pathological lesions from the Early Horizon burials, including periosteal reactions on a femur (A) and tibia (B), osteomyelitis on a radius (C), cribra orbitalia (D), porotic hyperostosis (E), and linear enamel hypoplasia (F).

and malnutrition (Table 3.1; Figures 3.1, 3.7). Periosteal reactions were most commonly experienced, with 13 of 35 individuals (37%) demonstrating these lesions (Figure 3.7a, 3.7b). One of these individuals had osteomyelitis (Figure 3.7c). Porotic lesions were also fairly common; 40% (8/20) of individuals had orbital lesions (Figure 3.7d) and 20% (7/35) had cranial lesions (Figure 3.7e). Finally, LEH were also fairly common (Figure 3.7f), impacting 24% (9/37) of individuals, the majority of whom (7/9) were juveniles. Lesions were overall evenly distributed between adult demographic groups, although male and probable male adults had more periosteal reactions, while female and probable female adults had more porotic lesions. One adult of indeterminate sex had both periosteal and porotic lesions. Juveniles had relatively high rates of porotic lesions (9/13 or 69%), which is not unexpected as this group is most likely to develop them due to the biological processes involved. Frequency of LEH was also high for juveniles (7/15 or 46%).

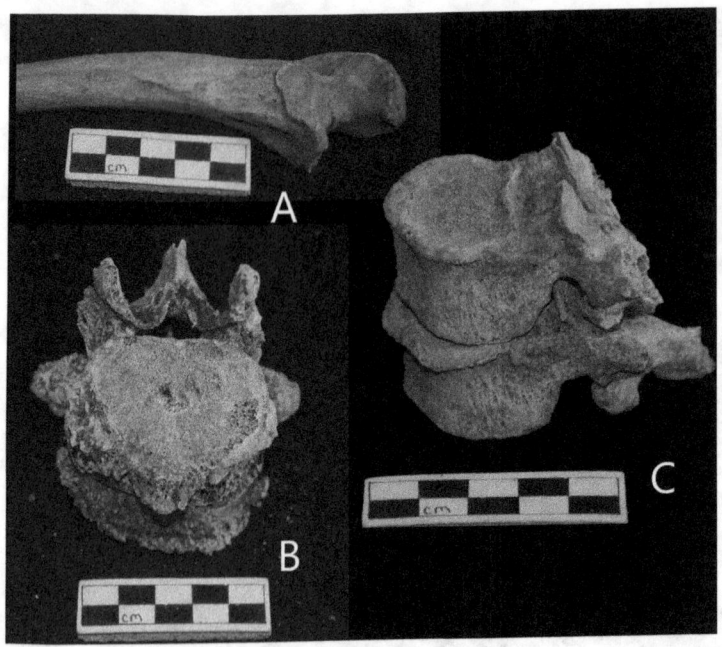

Figure 3.8 Examples of osteoarthritis from the Early Horizon burials, including pitting and lipping on the margin of the lunar notch of an ulna (A), lipping and a Schmorl's node on a lumbar vertebra (B), and lipping on two lumber vertebral bodies (C).

Osteoarthritis was observed at lower rates than during the Preceramic; however, certain OA was still consistently observed in the Early Horizon burial sample (Table 3.2; Figures 3.3, 3.8). Of 24 observable individuals, 15 (63%) presented shoulder and elbow OA Figure 3.8a) while only 2 (8%) presented hip and knee OA. Fifteen 21 (71%) observable individuals had degenerative vertebral ditions, including 3 individuals with Schmorl's nodes (Figure 3.8b, :). The low presentation of hip and knee arthritis is significantly than the Preceramic rate. However, two adolescents presented bral conditions and one young adult had already developed orl's nodes, suggesting that intense labor began at a fairly young steoarthritis did not vary statistically by estimated sex category. le isotope values from Early Horizon individuals generally ixed diets of C_3 and C_4 plants, and lacustrine and terres- ein sources (Figure 3.5). The Early Horizon carbon apatite mean reflects values consistent with Centroid 4, a 70:30 C_3:C_4 diet, with more than 65% of protein coming from C_3 sources (Figure 3.6) (Froehle et al. 2012). While C_3 resources still dominated the diet, there is clear inclusion of dietary C_4 in some form. Archaeological and paleobotanical remains suggest that people across the lake basin increasingly relied on horticultural products overall, supporting these isotopic findings of some C_4 plant consumption (Bruno and Whitehead 2003, Capriles et al. 2008, Capriles et al. 2014, Chávez and Thompson 2006). Alongside the plant domestication and cultivation that occurred during the Early Horizon, it seems as though people were occasionally using domesticated animals in addition to consuming fish for protein.

Nutrition and stress may have been an increasing problem for Early Horizon individuals, based on higher lesion rates, and more individuals with multiple conditions. This trend towards worsening health may be in part the results of diets shifting towards domesticated resources. In turning towards farming, Early Horizon groups limited their ability to capitalize on all the resources available in the lake basin, which may have elevated risk of shortages. Additionally, the variety of exploited resources was restricted, limiting the diversity of micronutrients in the diet. The cranial lesions associated with malnutrition are not clearly linked to any particular micronutrient, but instead indicate that multiple important minerals and vitamins (including iron and vitamin B12) were missing from the diet. Carbon values suggest that malnutrition may be linked to maize consumption, which entered the diet in limited amounts during the Early Horizon (Juengst et al. 2021). Maize is notoriously low in iron and vitamin B12 and actually blocks iron absorption unless eaten in combination with other foods high in niacin (Glahn et al. 2019; Walker et al. 2009). While it is unlikely that maize is the only cause for increasing malnutrition in the Early Horizon, it may have been part of the problem.

Adding to nutritional stress, Early Horizon peoples lived in permanent villages and increased their contact with domesticated animals, including camelids and guinea pigs. The periosteal reactions and LEH experienced by this group suggest that they were exposed to more pathogens and suffered from infectious disease more regularly. In fact, the rate of periosteal reactions observed for this group (37%) is higher than many other forager and agricultural Andean groups (Andrushko et al. 2006; Gómez Mejía 2012; Klaus and Tam 2009; Lowman, et al. 2019; Suby 2020; Ubelaker and Newson 2002; Williams and Murphy 2013). It seems likely that the sedentary settlements of Early Horizon peoples promoted waste accumulation that more mobile lifeways avoided, ultimately negatively impacting their overall health.

However, living in semi-to-fully sedentary villages may have reduced some types of bodily stress and strain, evidenced by the dramatic reduction of lower body osteoarthritis. Rates of OA reduced for all parts of the body, and significantly so for the hips and knees. Age increases the risk of developing OA; however, older adults in the Early Horizon had lower rates of arm OA than Preceramic older adults, and rates of Early Horizon leg OA was lower than both older and younger Preceramic individuals. This pattern suggests that the changes to OA are indeed at least partially related to lessened intensity in activity and labor during the Early Horizon.

Notably, no particular demographic group was particularly stressed nor at increased risk of disease compared with others. Labor also seems to have been fairly equitably distributed across the population, with some individuals suffering from OA but not patterned by sex or burial location. This is important because it indicates that during this period, social ranking was not yet present in these communities, in terms of limited access to food, increased labor demands, or negative health outcomes for certain segments of society. This is consistent with the lack of archaeological evidence for social stratification during this time. Interestingly, Logan et al. (2012) suggested that sharing maize beer (*chicha*) at temples on the Taraco Peninsula in the southern Titicaca Basin was central to ceremonies of ancestor veneration and likely worked to reinforce community bonds (Janusek 2008; Logan et al. 2012). The slight but notable amount of C_4 consumption during the EH may also be the result of sharing *chicha* at temple events; if this was occurring, it could have mitigated social tensions over access to resources and promoted communality between groups.

Stress, Labor, and Diet during the Early Intermediate Period

During the Early Intermediate Period, 51% (36/70) of individuals displayed some sort of skeletal stress lesion (Table 3.1; Figure 3.1, 3.9). The most common were porotic orbital lesions (53% or 18/34 observable individuals), followed by periosteal reactions (33% or 20/61 observable individuals) (Figure 3.9a, 3.9b). Twenty percent or 10/50 observable individuals had porotic hyperostosis (Figure 3.9c) and 7 percent (4/61) of individuals suffered from osteomyelitis (Figure 3.9b). Adults in all sex categories displayed periosteal reactions and cribra orbitalia, and all but indeterminate adults also had osteomyelitis and porotic hyperostosis. Female and probable female individuals were significantly more likely to display skeletal markers of stress (χ^2 (3, N = 70) = 10.1772, p = .017119) when compared with

Figure 3.9 Examples of pathological lesions from the EIP burials, including periosteal reactions on a tibia (A), osteomyelitis on a tibia (B), and pitting on the occipital bone of a juvenile individual (C).

other EIP adults. Juvenile remains most frequently presented orbital and cranial porotic lesions. Juvenile and young adult remains were statistically more common during this period as well, possibly related to these disease loads.

During the EIP, 21 of 35 (60%) observable individuals presented shoulder and elbow osteoarthritis, while 11 of 38 (29%) had degenerative changes to the hip and knee joints (Table 3.2; Figures 3.10a, 3.10b). Eighteen of 29 (62%) observable individuals presented vertebral degeneration, including two adults under 30 presented Schmorl's nodes (Figures 3.10c, 3.10d). Adults under 30 years of age at the time of death were slightly more likely to have vertebral lipping and other degenerative change than older adults, but this was not statistically significant. Rates of arm and vertebral OA were lower than previous periods overall, while hip and knee OA increased slightly. Evidence of OA or degenerative vertebral changes did not vary statistically by estimated sex category.

Similar to the Early Horizon, stable isotope values from EIP individuals reflect a mix of C_3 and C_4 resources (Table 3.3; Figures 3.5, 3.6). Interestingly, nitrogen values are significantly less enriched, suggesting a decline in protein consumption, or consumption of protein from lower trophic levels. The slightly wider carbon spacing

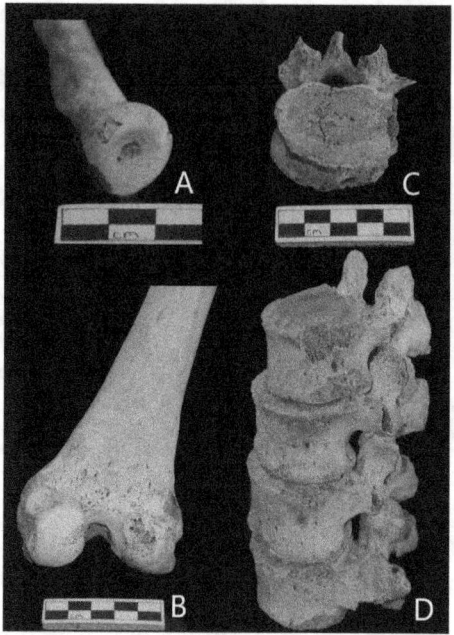

Figure 3.10 Examples of osteoarthritis from the EIP burials, including pitting on the edge of the head of a radius (A), eburnation and pitting on the distal condyle of a femur (B), lipping and compression of a lumbar vertebra (C), and lipping and pitting on thoracic and lumbar vertebral bodies (D).

indicates this may be linked to an increased reliance on terrestrial protein. Agricultural terraces expanded during the EIP; the isotope values here suggest that diets shifted with the landscape to a fuller reliance on these farmed land resources. Interestingly, this shift towards farmed resources also coincided with a dry period in the lake basin (Abbott et al. 1997; Juengst et al. 2021). Low or fluctuating lake levels seem to have prompted people to turn to land resources in order to have a stable food source. In fact, archaeological studies of faunal remains from the Taraco Peninsula show a dramatic decrease in fish remains during the EIP (Capriles et al. 2008; Moore 2011), corresponding nicely with the isotope values here.

While overall rates of pathological lesions and stable isotope values are not statistically different for this period, there were significantly more juvenile and young adults included in the EIP burial sample (Table 2.3). Preservation may be contributing to this trend as juvenile remains are less likely to preserve than adult skeletons. However, both Ch'isi and Muruqullu had stone-lined tombs, so preservation should have been similar between the sites. Additionally, the increase in young adults remains is notable as young adults in particular should be generally more able to respond to immune insults than the extremely young or elderly. More young adults and older juveniles dying during this period could also be related to increases in fertility, that overall the population was larger and thus there were simply more people around (Wood et al. 1992). While this cannot be entirely ruled out, the connection with persistent pathology associated with malnutrition and disease suggests that bodily stress may have been extreme during this period.

There are also significant changes in female/probable female adult experiences of stress and protein consumption. This could also partially be an issue of preservation as female and probable female remains were less prevalent than male, probable male, unsexed adult, or non-adult remains overall. Yet, that 9 of 10 female or probable female individuals presented some evidence of stress likely indicates that there was some elevated risk for identities linked to being biologically female during this time. This may have been linked to the changes in protein consumption—while females and probable female adults are not isotopic outliers, perhaps the new dietary pattern exacerbated underlying conditions for these individuals.

The combination of a drought, increased investment in ritual architecture, increased bodily stress, and differential life experiences of females suggests that social ranking may have developed during the EIP. However, this potential inequality does not seem to have translated into increased labor, as rates of OA were generally lower than early periods (with the exception of hip and knee OA) and were not more likely to impact certain groups based on sex or burial location. Changing environmental circumstances likely limited what resources were available, providing an opportunity for male individuals to claim privileged access, perhaps by manipulating previously established ritual power. Other indicators of status differentiation (rates of violent injury, social networks, etc.), explored in subsequent chapters, will help elucidate this pattern.

Connections with Larger Social, Economic, and Ecological Changes

Combining analysis of pathological lesions and stable isotopes, we can note some interesting trends over time. The frequencies of periosteal reactions and porotic hyperostosis remained remarkably consistent over time, suggesting that experiences of disease and stress did not dramatically fluctuate when considering the burial groups overall (although the increase in young adults during the EIP hints at increasing stress in the later periods). Degenerative joint disease and osteoarthritis rates for shoulder and elbow joints and the vertebral column also remain fairly consistent over time, decreasing most notably in the Early Horizon. Osteoarthritis in the hip and knee dropped dramatically after the Preceramic, perhaps related to changes in subsistence strategy that required less intense long-distance running or walking.

The stable isotope data also shows that in general, diets did not fluctuate dramatically overtime, with regular consumption of C_3 plants, fish, and occasional inclusion of C_4 plants during all time periods. However, when considering rates of pathological lesions by demographic category, it becomes clear that certain groups were more at risk of disease than others were. In particular, females and probable females during the EIP were at significantly higher risk of developing lesions associated with stress and disease, perhaps associated with the decrease in protein consumption noted during this period. In the next chapter, we'll explore how these individuals were linked socially—perhaps familial lineage and homeland promoted health and access to good foods for some while leaving others in the lurch.

4 Creating Relationships
Family and Friends

Social networks are key to any human society; these networks are often the basis for how we organize our families, access resources, and structure power dynamics. Humans create these networks in numerous ways, by drawing on many identity markers and characteristics such as symbolic and biological kinship, spatial proximity, shared belief systems, and others (Anderson 1983; Johnson and Paul 2016; Sahlins 2013). This chapter will investigate how our bodies record these traits over the life course, in particular how our biological relationships and physical location on the landscape link us into social networks from the moment of our birth.

Biological Kinship and Bioarchaeology

Community structures are often related to ancestry and reproductive relationships; in fact, "family" may be one of the most fundamental social units across human cultures (Deloria 1944; Evans-Pritchard 1951; Fei 1939; Johnson and Paul 2016; Mead 1934). Families are responsible for teaching offspring social values, organizing daily practices, and are often key to determining in-group membership, as well as incorporating new members through marriage. This "kin identity" is inherently collective, uniting people by shared experiences through ancestry, domestic space, and/or other marker of relatedness (McKinnon 1991) However, how humans define who is related varies broadly. Many families and kinship practices include people both biologically related and related through some other mechanism, termed "alternative" or "fictive" kin (Gregoricka 2013; Gregoricka et al. 2020; Pilloud and Larsen 2011). Effectively, kinship establishes one's first collective identity as humans are born into these relationships often before they can choose for themselves (Barth 1969).

DOI: 10.4324/9781003175971-4

While kinship does not require biological ties, the needs of human infants necessitate extended and intimate parenting, which often creates strong ties between parents and offspring (although this often includes adoptive and surrogate parents as well as those who are biologically related) (Gellar 2009; Maestripieri 1999; Sahlins 2013; Smith 2009). Social relationships involving procreation are the basis for kinship among many human groups, and biogenetically related individuals often share some collective identity (Kent and Johnson 2016; Sahlins 2013; Shapiro 2014; Smith 2009; Mead 1934). So, kinship is complicated as it is both a biological and cultural process (Ottenheimer 1995; Sahlins 2013).

In the Andes, kinship practices include genetic and non-genetic family members through extended and local networks, most often linked to a common ancestor (Abercrombie 1998; Goldstein 2000; Janusek 2008; Murra 1980; Van Vleet 2009). These networks inform daily activities and tasks such as subsistence tasks and house chores, and guide large decisions about career, marriage, and child-rearing (among others) (Van Vleet 2009). Central to family today, these networks are traceable into the past, and while archaeological kinship is often hard to identify, it is clear that past Andean peoples often practiced similar kinship strategies (Bray 2015; Goldstein 2000; Janusek 2008; Murra 1980). Past Andean kinship networks were often determined by the historical and genealogical relationship to a real or fictive ancestor, rather than based purely on spatial geographies. Additionally, marriage and reproduction tended to be endogamous, as kinship structured social roles and mapped community affiliation (Goldstein 2003:184).

Thus, Andean people from the same kinship group would display similar genetic markers, especially when compared to multiethnic communities. Genetic relationships expressed in phenotype can help archaeologists recreate genetic and community relationships. This offers important data for recreating past community structure, given that community members are often both social and biological kin (Stojanowski and Buikstra 2004). While measuring phenotypic expression of genetic relationships is not a perfect measure of community, it can be the first step to outlining social relationships, especially when combined with markers of social affiliation such as burial location and associated material goods.

Biodistance analysis estimates how closely related different populations were, based on prevalence of certain morphological traits. The basic premise is the morphology of certain biological traits is determined hereditarily, thus populations that are closely related should have phenotypes that look similar when compared to those of groups less closely related. These calculations include within and between group variation (Stojanowski and Buikstra 2004). Skeletal and dental traits that are inherited can be used to determine these relationships. Observation of these traits produces a record of shared population traits, which can be statistically analyzed to show outliers within a population (Scott and Turner 1988; Stojanowski and Buikstra 2004; Sutter and Cortez 2005; Sutter and Verano 2006) as well as different morphological compositions between groups (Konigsberg 1990).

Mobility and Physical Proximity

While physical proximity is certainly not the only delineation of communities and kinship, the idea of "natural communities" relies heavily on proximity (Yaeger and Canuto 2000). While Andean kinship did not always rely on proximity for inclusion, people that live near each other often engage in trade as a way to access necessary food items and other material goods. Along with material goods, these relationships can also contribute to the trade of ideas, practices, and beliefs. Modern potters in the northern Titicaca Basin regularly trade with neighboring towns as they all have become experts in one or two steps of the potting process, that is, clay collection, molding forms, firing large/small pots, and decoration. While each village maintains a local identity, they are closely linked to their neighbors to form a larger potting community (Chávez, K. 1992).

Conversely, sometimes communities are not limited to direct neighbors. In the Andes, families often extended vertically along mountainsides in order to gain access to multiple different ecozones. For instance, having a relative in a lower ecozone may provide access to goods such as chili peppers to those people living in higher regions, who may trade for these items with llama wool and potatoes (Goldstein 2000; Janusek 2008; Murra 1980, 1985; Sutter 2000). Family communities were thus somewhat spread out across the landscape and likely through different geologic zones. In this geographic pattern, even distant family members would return to their natal homeland community fairly regularly, maintaining what Yaeger and Canuto call "frequent co-presence" (2000:6). In this way, geographic distance does not necessarily correlate directly with community relationships.

Movement of people in the Andes has also been caused by processes unrelated to community or in fact, due to a breakdown or upheaval of community. The Inka Empire regularly relocated large portions of conquered communities, in order to weaken social ties and manipulate labor (Covey 2000, 2006; Hu and Quave 2020; Sutter 2000). Under the control of some Andean states, Wari, Tiwanaku, and Moche, people moved around considerable regions, as they created colonies, expanded into new areas, and developed elaborate trade networks (Goldstein 2003; Knudson 2004; Knudson and Tung 2011). Finally, during times of war, people were occasionally captured and brought to sacred locations to be sacrificed or held captive (Sutter and Cortez 2005; Sutter and Verano 2006). Sometimes people who were buried near each other may have lived or originated from much further away and relocated either through force or choice.

Bioarchaeology can test geographic relationships of past peoples through strontium isotope studies. Strontium isotope ratios ($^{87}Sr/^{86}Sr$) vary according to local geology. ^{87}Sr is a product of ^{87}Rb decay, therefore the $^{87}Sr/^{86}Sr$ ratio in a rock is a function of the initial $^{87}Sr/^{86}Sr$, the Rb/Sr ratio, and the age of the rock. In general, continental rocks such as shales and granites tend to have high Rb/Sr and high $^{87}Sr/^{86}Sr$ ratios (typically above 0.710), in contrast to volcanic rocks such as basalts and andesites that tend to have low Rb/Sr and low $^{87}Sr/^{86}Sr$ ratios (typically below 0.707). Local geologic strontium leaches into drinking water, and is incorporated principally into plants (producers) and consumer (animal) tissue, including human bone and tooth enamel, by substitution of strontium for calcium in biogenic hydroxyapatite (bioapatite).

If a person consumes predominantly local water and food over the course of their childhood development and lifetime, their dental and skeletal strontium ratios should reflect the local bioavailable strontium (Ericson 1985; Knudson 2004, 2008; Price et al. 2002; Sharpe et al. 2018; Slovak and Paytan 2011; Valentine et al. 2008). In human tooth enamel, strontium reflects the region where one lived during childhood and adolescence since adult dental enamel is fully formed by 10–15 years of age (Hillson 2008; Slovak and Paytan 2011). Strontium in bone reflects where one lived during the last decade or so prior to death, as bony tissue regenerates continually (Knudson 2004, 2008). Dental enamel is ideal for this test as it is resistant to diagenetic contamination, especially compared to bone (Knudson 2004; Waldron et al. 1979). Because strontium ratios in dental enamel reflect where one lived in their early years, any ratios outside of the Titicaca range will indicate immigrants to the area.

Strontium in the lake basin stems from the lake basin geology and through inflow from the five major rivers. The local geology of the basin and the river beds include a mix of Cenozoic sediments from the uplifted central Andean fold of the Eastern Cordillera and modern volcanic contributions from the Western Cordillera, in addition to

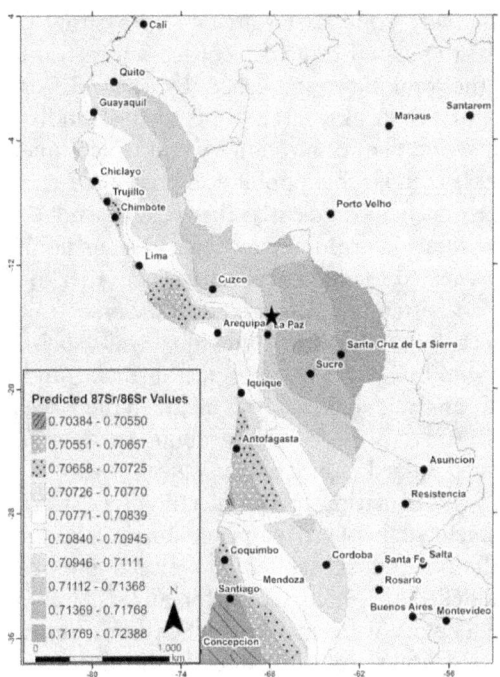

Figure 4.1 Predicted strontium map for Peru and Bolivia (adapted from Scaffidi and Knudson 2020).

occasional Tertiary sandstones and argillite (Baucom and Rigsby 1999; Grove et al. 2003; Marc-Antoine et al. 2021). These values are averaged in lake water; a modern surface water sample of Lago Chuicuito returned an $^{87}Sr/^{86}Sr$ value of 0.708215 (Grove et al. 2003). However, this does vary by local region in the basin. For example, modern water samples from the Rio Coata in the northern basin and Rio Ilave in the western basin return values below 0.707300, while samples from Rio Suches and Rio Huaycho in the eastern basin are above 0.709700 (Grove et al. 2003: 284). Generally, $^{87}Sr/^{86}Sr$ signatures interpreted as local to the lake basin are considered to range from 0.708300 through 0.701100 (Figure 4.1) (Knudson 2008; Scaffidi and Knudson 2020).

Biodistance Methods and Results

Nonmetric dental traits, one body of biodistance data, were observed for 153 individuals from five burial groups: Ch'isi, Qopakati,

Muruqullu, Tawa Qeñani, and Cundisa. Results at two levels, individual and all burials, were compared statistically to show correlation and agreement of the dental traits. I recorded nonmetric dental variation, following the rankings established by the ASU Dental Morphology System (Turner et al. 1991). I included all individuals with observable permanent dentition, complete and incomplete, in order to have the largest comparable population possible. I excluded deciduous teeth and extremely worn teeth as they often do not present the same types of variation or are unobservable. Certain nonmetric dental traits were also selected for statistical analysis in order to avoid the biases described by Sutter and Cortez (2005). Some traits are highly correlated with each other or other individual traits such as sex and are therefore not good markers of biological distance, and were thus excluded from this analysis. This analysis included the same traits as Sutter and Cortez (2005) to preserve comparability between studies as this is now a general standard in bioarchaeological research.

Statistical analyses for calculating biodistance involve establishing the correlation or agreement between pairs of individuals, first for a single burial population and subsequently between populations. Individuals were included if they had scores for at least five of the dental traits scored and pairs were included when both individuals had scores for matching dental traits. Subsequently, the scores for each pair were averaged across the population to see group cohesion for a single burial population. Outliers with little agreement with any other individual in the population were also noted. Each population was compared with every other burial group in turn.

At the population level, these results show that overall, most groups in the study were closely related biologically. Agreement equal to or above 0.5 indicates close correlation and little disagreement between individuals overall. I found that all groups agreed with themselves (little intragroup diversity or variability of dental traits) and with other burial groups (little intergroup diversity or variability of dental traits) (Table 4.1). The only exception to this was the comparison with Muruqullu to Ch'isi and Muruqullu to itself, when the correlation analysis results were slightly below 0.5 (0.4852 and 0.466 respectively). This may reflect the inclusion of the Preceramic individuals in the Muruqullu burial sample—these individuals from an earlier period may have been more distantly related than those during the Early Horizon and Early Intermediate Period. However, these results are so close to the agreement cutoff, it is unlikely that they reflect significant results and may alternatively be caused by variability in sample size for each burial group (Chris Weisen personal communication 2014).

Table 4.1 Biodistance analysis where agreement equal to or above 0.5 indicates close correlation

Sites	Ch'isi	Qopakati	Cundisa	Muruqullu	Tawa Qeñani
Ch'isi	0.501095	0.581135	0.579764	0.485184	0.551893
Qopakati		0.561033	0.611908	0.529832	0.620498
Cundisa			0.640318	0.534398	0.685551
Muruqullu				0.465956	0.616989
Tawa Qeñani					0.833898

Strontium Isotope Results

Teeth from 40 individuals excavated from the Copacabana Peninsula were tested in order to see the geographic origins of these individuals. Of the 40 samples tested, 36 were from EIP contexts, two were from Early Horizon contexts and two from Preceramic contexts. Overall, the majority of individuals (29/40) fell within the Titicaca Basin range (0.7083–0.7110), including individuals from all age ranges and estimated sex categories. However, eight individuals fell clearly outside of this range and were classified as nonlocal, while three individuals were just below the lower end of the local range and classified as semi-local (Figure 4.2). Seven nonlocals were EIP individuals, one nonlocal was from an Early Horizon context, and one semi-local individual was from a Preceramic context. While the burials tested were strongly skewed towards the EIP (36/40 samples), there was at least one nonlocal or semi-local individual from each time period, indicating that semi-regular long-distance travel was enduring practice in the lake basin.

Eight individuals buried at three different sites clearly had nonlocal signatures. This included three adults, one adolescent, and four juveniles. Of the adults and adolescent, three were estimated to be female while sex could not be estimated for the fourth individual. The nonlocal signatures stemming from juvenile individuals likely reflect the geologic circumstances during gestation, as those teeth developed enamel in utero. The adult signatures reflect conditions of middle and late childhood, as the second and third molars developed.

Three individuals (two adults of indeterminate sex and one female adult) were classified as semi-local, as their signatures placed them below the Titicaca Basin mean but within the standard of error. This may indicate regular movement in and out of the lake basin. Alternatively, these borderline signatures could indicate regular

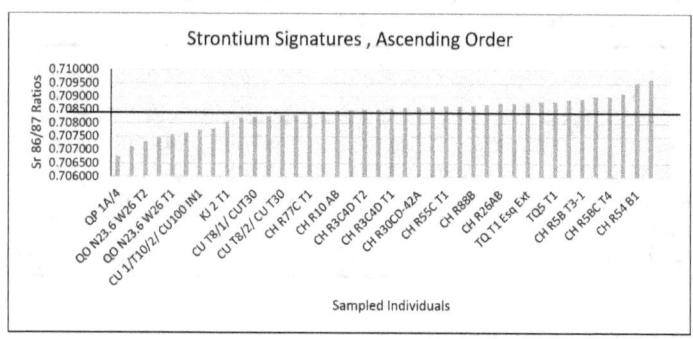

Figure 4.2 Strontium isotope ratios for 40 sampled individuals. Black bar indicates the average minimum strontium ratio for the Titicaca Basin.

consumption of nonlocal foods, which would also impact strontium signatures.

There is quite a range of nonlocal signatures, from 0.706737 to 0.70777. All fall below the Titicaca Basin average range and could reflect a variety of areas around the Andes, mostly associated with the geologically younger regions, such as the coastal valleys of Peru and Chile (Figure 4.1) (Scaffidi and Knudson 2020). In particular, the 0.7067 signature correlates with the Moquegua Valley, where later lake basin peoples developed important trade and kinship connections. However, complicating the picture, modern water samples from the northern Rio Coata and western Rio Ilave in the Titicaca Basin also return values in this range (Grove et al. 2003: 284), likely due to the presence of volcanic rock. It is possible that Copacabana "travelers" could be from these nearby regions, rather than the Moquegua Valley or other areas of the coast.

Migrants and Family

Analysis of biological kinship and residential mobility suggests some interesting social patterns during the Preceramic, Early Horizon, and EIP. Though people were moving to the lake basin later in life, none of the nonlocal or semi-local individuals were biodistance outliers, suggesting that they were biologically related to people living in the lake basin. Additionally, these biological ties persisted throughout time, as individuals from the Preceramic, Early Horizon, and EIP generally did not strongly differ from each other. One exception to this are the Preceramic individuals buried at Muruqullu who cluster more tightly with each other than with others buried at the site and are more distantly related to those from later time periods. However, overall, the differences in phenotypic dental traits were not statistically different between individuals or burial locations. While migration to and around the lake basin was occurring, it is clear that people typically reproduced with others who shared many biological traits, perhaps suggesting broadly endogamous reproductive patterns.

People of all ages moved prior to death, spending their childhoods and gestational periods away from the Copacabana Peninsula. Because adult molars reflect the geologic environment of middle to late childhood and deciduous dentition reflects gestational geologic environments, it seems that most nonlocal individuals moved later in life, after childhood and/or pregnancy. It is unclear if the juveniles themselves were born in different regions or if their gestational parent moved late in pregnancy. Either way, it seems that some adults buried on the Copacabana Peninsula spent their childhoods and early adolescence in other areas of the Andes or lake basin, or were buried far from home.

All nonlocal and semi-local adults were estimated to be female or of indeterminate sex. It is possible (even likely) that male-identified individuals also regularly moved between regions, but it seems that something about having less testosterone meant one was more likely to relocate between regions during reproductive years. Notably, nonlocal individuals did not differ patterns of disease, diet, trauma nor cranial modification style (see Chapters 3 and 5), indicating that their embodied identities were not necessarily distinctive from local individuals.

While strontium isotopes appear to divide individuals buried on the Copacabana Peninsula into "local/nonlocal," it seems likely that these categories were not salient for people's lived experiences of community. Beyond the biogeochemical signature, nothing marked "nonlocal" individuals as different in any way. In fact, despite living elsewhere during their early lives, these individuals were not genetically distant, suggesting long-distance reproductive networks extended through several regions during the Early Horizon and EIP. However, inclusivity of geographically disparate individuals may not necessarily indicate a lack of hierarchy or social ranking. The next chapter considers two additional lines of evidence, trauma and cranial modification, to see how people experienced those aspects of identity during this time.

5 Growing Divisions
Violence and Identity

Delineating in-group from out-group is an important and common human action (Barth 1969). Accordingly, people often mark their identities in salient and visible ways, communicating quickly with others about their social affiliations. While this often provides advantages of inclusion, highly visible identity markers may also be a liability if individuals find themselves in different social contexts, particularly if the identity marker is a permanent and immutable modification to the body.

In the Andes, heads are and were symbolically important and visible signifiers of identity and power, manipulated in various ways among the living and the dead to communicate affiliation, status, and inclusion (Arnold and Hastorf 2008; Torres-Rouff 2002). One common Andean practice marking identity was cranial modification—the intentional shaping of the skull into elongated or flattened shapes. Practiced from at least 6000 BC through the early seventeenth century (Friede 1965), artificially modified crania were linked to status, lineage, and ethnic group by many Andean cultures (Blom 2005a, 2005b; Hoshower et al. 1995; Lozada and Buikstra 2002; Okumura 2014; Torres-Rouff 2002, 2020; Velasco 2018). The meanings of modification across the Andes are difficult to identify, as the motivations for this practice were variable and locally contingent (Mannheim et al. 2018). But in all circumstances, cranial modification acted to bond diverse social groups, masking heterogeneous life experiences with a shared cranial shape (Pechenkina and Delgado 2006; Velasco 2018).

While cranial modification may have brought people together in some circumstances, this highly visible marker of identity could also potentially be a liability, marking one as belonging to a certain group when one was in foreign territory. In landscapes of social violence, having a modified cranium or a specific type of modification could

DOI: 10.4324/9781003175971-5

have elevated one's risk of trauma and/or stigmatization. While we often think of violence as disorderly, people can use violence as a part of social control, in an effort to *maintain* order. This is because violence also has the "ability to unite, create stability, and be progressive" (Pérez 2012:14), simultaneously with having negative impacts on others. Through violent actions, the traumatized and not-traumatized may be on display and readily identifiable, acting as a reminder about appropriate behaviors, social roles, and access to power. Thus, violence is often critical to maintenance of community systems, as an inclusive and exclusive force.

This chapter explores rates of cranial modification and frequency of skeletal trauma on the Copacabana Peninsula in order to understand if and how visibly marked identities were linked to social categories and violent behaviors for Copacabana peoples over time. Given the changing socio-economic landscape, community relationships may have become strained, and people may have established new mechanisms for navigating these interactions. Did cranial modification increase over time, as people created new in-groups and out-groups? Did violence increase as a result of socio-economic changes or as cranial modification styles developed and changed and people could readily identify those who belonged to a different group?

Identity and Cranial Modification

Andean peoples modified the crania of children in order to mark identity, ethnic affiliation, social class, and power (Blom 2005a, 2005b; Okumura 2014; Torres-Rouff 2002). Skulls of infants were molded through the use of boards, bindings, and even hands, into elongated, erect, or flattened shapes (de la Vega 1966 [1609]; Diez de San Miguel 1964 [1567]; Torres-Rouff 2002). While the exact meanings of these modifications varied over time and space, cranial modification was clearly linked to important identity categories such as ethnic group or natal community.

Cranial modification necessarily occurs during infancy because the cranial bones fuse throughout the juvenile period. This timing of the practice is important because it means caretakers choose to modify an infant's head and in what style, and because the modification is subsequently unchangeable (Blom 2005b; Tiesler 2013; Torres-Rouff 2002, 2020; Torres-Rouff and Knudson 2017). Thus, cranial modification fundamentally does not reflect the decisions, identity or status of the adult individual bearing the modification. Rather, it reflects the decision, identity or statuses of the individual's kin or community. If

68 *Growing Divisions: Violence and Identity*

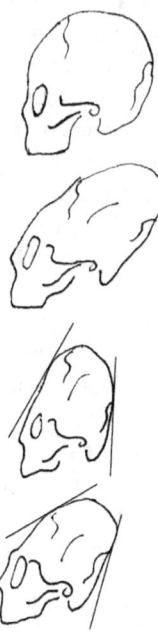

Figure 5.1 Simplified types of cranial modification in the Andes. Top to bottom: unmodified, oblique, erect type 1, erect type 2.

a modified individual encounters another group or relocates to a new area, their head shape may continually mark them as a member of their natal community if modification type varies. This highly visible and unchangeable marker of identity could thus make individuals targets of exclusion or inclusion when outside their natal communities or interacting with people of other ethnic groups.

Different forms of cranial modification existed in the Andes, recorded by Spanish chroniclers and ethnohistorians, and categorized today based on the cranial form observed by bioarchaeologists (Figure 5.1) (Blom 2005a; Cieza de León 1984 [1553]:124; de la Vega 1966 [1609]; Diez de San Miguel 1964 [1567]; Hoshower et al. 1995; Torres-Rouff 2020). Methods of cataloging cranial modification vary; however, most studies broadly identify two main types: tabular or annular (originally defined by Argentinian anthropologist José Imbelloni) (Dembo and Imbelloni 1938). These may be subsequently subdivided to reflect the degree of modification or regional variations (Allison et al. 1981; Blom 2005a; Pomeroy et al. 2010). In general, tabular and annular modification assess methods of achieving head shape and are generally recognized as resulting from the use of boards or cords, respectively (O'Brien and Stanley 2013; Torres-Rouff 2020).

Tabular modification involves binding the cranium between two hard surfaces placed on the frontal and occipital bones. This can result in two styles: tabular erect and tabular oblique. In tabular erect modification, the cranium is flattened front to back, resulting in bulging parietals and an occipital at a 90° angle with the basicranium. Tabular oblique modification flattens the skull posteriorly, creating an obtuse angle between the occipital and basicranium (Kuzminsky et al. 2016; Torres-Rouff 2002). Annular modification is created by tightly wrapping the skull with cloth or cords, placing equal pressure around the skull, resulting in an elongated skull, with a sloped forehead (Blom 2005a; Kuzminsky et al. 2016; Torres-Rouff 2002).

Differentiating between tabular and annular modification often relies on impressions left behind by the pads or cords used. However, not all modifications clearly indicate one device or another. This complicates identification of type and often creates confusion between annular and tabular oblique forms. Thus, when binding device impressions are not observable, it may be more accurate to describe modification based on the angle of the frontal and occipital, as erect, oblique, or unmodified (Velasco 2018).

Violence and Identity

Violence can be defined as "an act of physical hurt deemed legitimate by the performer and illegitimate by (some) witness" (Riches 1986:8), and has long played an essential role in human society, particularly in the context of social inequality (Harrod and Martin 2014). Violence occurs within a variety of cultural contexts, and is ascribed meaning based on those settings; importantly, not all *harmful* behavior is inherently seen as violent (Pérez 2012). Additionally, while the above definition highlights physical harm, violence can also be inflicted on individuals and groups in psychological, social, and structural ways (Farmer 2003; Scheper-Hughes and Bourgois 2004). Ultimately, violent actions can be seen as performance, meant to instruct, unite, punish, control, and otherwise communicate salient social information to those within the cultural setting (Pérez 2012; Whitehead 2005).

In some circumstances, violent behaviors are enacted against outsiders, dividing peoples seen as local from those from different regions, communities, or social classes. Formal warfare, regular raids, and the creation of formal military forces may help to delineate groups, as people clearly fight for one side or another (Arkush and Allen 2006; Arkush and Tung 2013; Tung 2012; Worne et al. 2012). Violence against those seen as "other" and demonstrations of military reinforce these divisions as physical trauma or other kinds of deprivation are enacted against certain groups, but not everyone. These types of violent conflict often increase during times of environmental stress and associated socioeconomic changes because responding to local ecological changes and new social environments may involve increased competition over resources, conquests of new territories, or stricter adherence to boundaries between groups (Juengst 2020; Kuckelman 2012; Montgomery and Perry 2012; Redfern 2020).

Violence can also become normalized in order to protect a local in-group, maintain social hierarchies, and target members within society in socially-sanctioned ways (Buzon and Richman 2007; Farmer 1999, 2003; Martin et al. 2012; Pérez 2012; Redfern and Chamberlain 2011; Tung 2007, 2008; Wakely 1996; Walker 2001; Wheeler et al. 2013). In cases of normalized violence, the idea of a victim is removed from the encounter, creating the illusion that violence has not occurred despite bodily and emotional trauma (Krohn-Hansen 1994). This may occur through selection of certain individuals for ritual events such as sacrifice or cannibalism (Duncan 2012; Hatch 2012). More commonly, practices such as corporal punishment and domestic abuse (Tung 2008; Wheeler et al. 2013) or neglect, malnutrition, and unequal access to resources (Farmer 2003; Klaus 2012) are routes to normalize violence within society.

Both normalized and abnormal violent encounters can result in trauma to the skeleton, allowing bioarchaeologists to partially reconstruct the events leading up to the broken bone or otherwise altered body (Buzon and Richman 2007; Tung 2007, 2008; Wakely 1996; Walker 1997, 2001). For instance, facial or cranial trauma often results from face-to-face, interpersonal conflict, as the head and face are highly symbolic targets and trauma to these areas can be quite painful. Cranial trauma can of course also result from accidents (i.e., falling down stairs) but forensic studies show that the location and nature of accidental cranial trauma are different from fractures resulting from conflict (Ehrlich and Maxeiner 2002; Kremer et al. 2008). In general, cranial fractures above "the hat-brim line," the widest circumference of the head, are linked to interpersonal conflict while those lower are

Growing Divisions: Violence and Identity 71

linked to falls. Variables such as intoxication and objects impeding a fall complicate this pattern, but across a large sample, blows are still mostly to cause trauma to the crown of the head (Kremer et al. 2008). Postcranial trauma can also indicate the circumstances leading up to the fracture. Like cranial trauma, fractures to the lower arm and ribs may result from an attack or from falling. And again, the location of lower arm fracture (on the mid arm vs. the wrist) may indicate defensive behavior to ward off a blow (mid-arm "parry" fractures) or crushing damage from catching yourself during a fall (lower wrist Colles' fractures) (Judd 2008; Walker 2001). The patterning of these injuries and correlation with other skeletal trauma can help distinguish between the two events. Moreover, the frequencies of certain kinds of trauma in a population can serve as indicators of violence. By recording and analyzing patterns of injury, we can establish if certain demographics were at higher risk of sustaining intentional injury (Berryman and Haun 1996; Brickley 2006; Judd 2008; Lovell 1997; Martin and Frayer 1997; Martin et al. 2012; Walker 1997, 2001).

Trauma and Cranial Modification Over Time

The Preceramic Period

All observable Preceramic individuals displayed erect cranial modification (4/4) (Table 5.1; Figures 5.2, 5.3). This included two male young adults, one male mature adult, and one probable male mature adult. Unfortunately, no individuals estimated to be female, probable female, or of indeterminate sex were observable for cranial modification, so it is unclear whether this modification was linked to sex categories.

Three (21%) of fourteen Preceramic individuals suffered from skeletal trauma (Table 5.1; Figures 5.4, 5.5). One (17%) of six suffered from cranial trauma, while two (14%) of fourteen had postcranial trauma. Cranial trauma included a healed sharp-force fracture to the

Table 5.1 Frequency of cranial modification types and trauma by time period

	Oblique Modification	Erect Modification	Unmodified Crania	Trauma
Preceramic	0/3	3/3	0/3	3/14 (21%)
EH	2/12 (16%)	3/12 (25%)	7/12 (58%)	1/39 (3%)
EIP	6/24 (25%)	5/24 (21%)	13/24 (54%)	10/58 (17%)
	8/29 (21%)	11/39 (28%)	20/39 (51%)	14/110 (13%)

Table 5.2 Connections between cranial modification and trauma by time period

Period	Modification Style	With Cranial Trauma	With Postcranial Trauma	Without Trauma
PC	Oblique	NA	NA	NA
	Erect	1/3	1/3	1/3
	Unmodified	NA	NA	NA
	Unobservable	0	1	10/11
EH	Oblique	0	0	2/2
	Erect	0	0	3/3
	Unmodified	1/7	0	6/7
EIP	Oblique	2/6	1/6	3/6
	Erect	3/5	0/5	2/5
	Unmodified	0/24	3/24	21/24

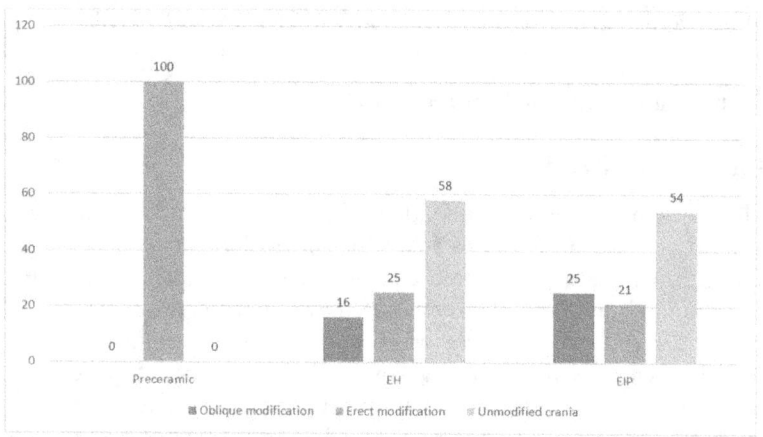

Figure 5.2 Percent of burial samples that displayed cranial modification for each time period.

frontal of a male young adult individual (Figure 5.5a). Postcranial trauma included an antemortem ulna fracture on a female mature adult (Figure 5.5b) and an extremely well healed humeral fracture on a probable male mature adult.

Trauma and cranial modification overlapped for two individuals: the young adult male with sharp-force cranial trauma and the humeral fracture on the probable male mature adult (Table 5.2). Two modified

Growing Divisions: Violence and Identity 73

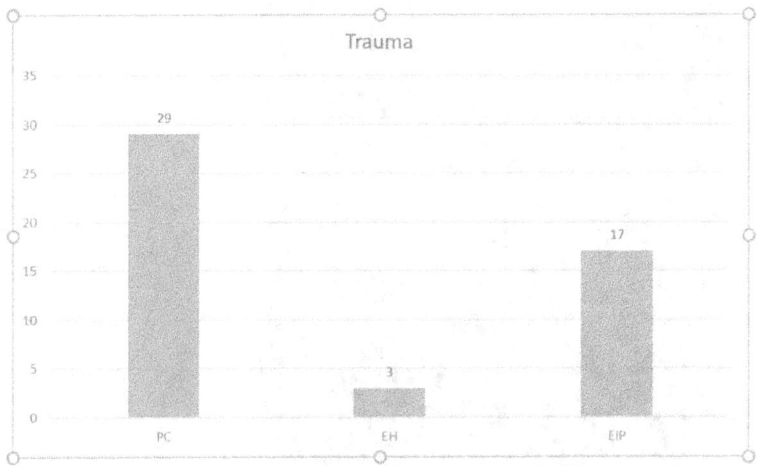

Figure 5.3 Percent of burial samples that displayed skeletal trauma for each time period.

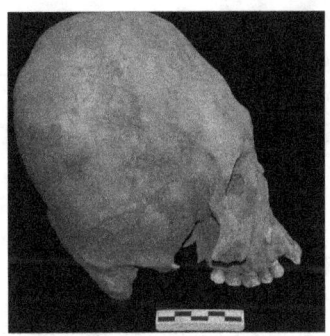

Figure 5.4 Example of erect cranial modification from the Preceramic.

individuals did not suffer any skeletal trauma. The female individual with the ulnar fracture was unobservable for cranial modification.

Preceramic individuals practiced erect cranial modification, as reflected by the examples given here. These examples all come from male or probable male individuals, as no other individuals had complete enough crania to observe cranial modification. While this limits the ability to understand how cranial modification related to lived

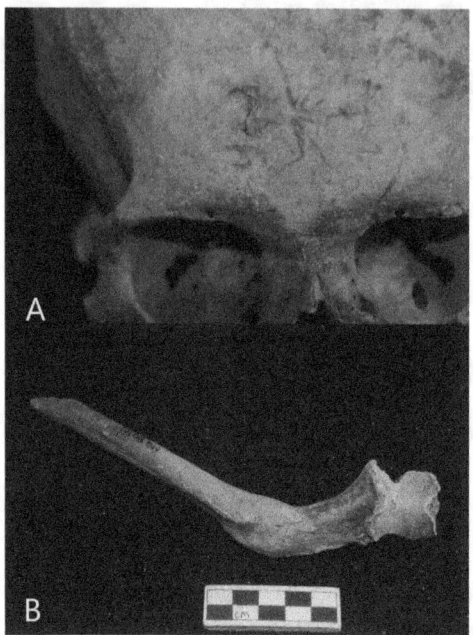

Figure 5.5 Examples of skeletal trauma from the Preceramic, including healed sharp-force trauma to the frontal bone (A) and a healed ulna fracture (B).

experience of identity as related to biological indicators of sex, it is interesting to note that the modification that does exist is relatively uniform in appearance.

Trauma was also relatively common for this burial group, with three individuals experiencing some sort of trauma. One of the wounds was healed sharp-force trauma to the frontal bone, likely produced by a stone projectile or other pointed weapon. This was almost certainly the result of interpersonal conflict and intentional violence (although it is possible that a hunting accident occurred). The healed ulnar fracture also suggests violence, as this type of fracture is commonly associated with defensive postures. While the other arm fracture likely resulted from a fall or other high impact accident, the combination of cranial trauma and a defensive wound suggests that Preceramic peoples did occasionally engage in face-to-face violent conflicts. Notably, both individuals survived their trauma long enough for the skeletal fractures to heal. While healing can happen in the absence of care-taking, the sharp-force trauma to the frontal bone would likely have incapacitated that individual at least briefly, suggesting that other Preceramic people took care of them after the injury. The ulnar fracture healed poorly, offset at a nearly 45-degree angle from the original alignment of the bone. This individual likely had limited use of that arm for the rest of their life, possibly requiring assistance with certain tasks (although arthritic changes to the elbow and wrist suggest that movement was still in fact possible).

Unfortunately, because of the limited sample, it is hard to correlate trauma and cranial modification. Speculatively, there appears to be a pattern of in-group identity importance, that having a modified cranium was necessary for belonging but also clearly visibly marked that belonged to a *particular* group. Perhaps visibly marking your identity as part of the group simultaneously signaled belonging in some social contexts while marking you as a target in others.

The Early Horizon

Twelve individuals were observed for cranial modification; of these, two displayed oblique modification while three displayed erect modification (Table 5.1; Figure 5.2, Figure 5.6). The remaining seven individuals had unmodified crania. Individuals with oblique modification included one male young adult and one probable male old adult. Individuals with erect modification included two probable male young adults and one female mature adult. Unmodified individuals included four juveniles, two probable male young adults, and one probable female young adult.

One (3%) of 39 observable individuals experienced trauma during the Early Horizon, a single instance of cranial trauma (Figures 5.4, 5.7). This was a perimortem frontal fracture on a juvenile individual. This individual did not display cranial modification. Accordingly, no individuals with cranial modification displayed skeletal trauma and vice versa.

During the Early Horizon, cranial modification diversity increased, while trauma rates plummeted (Table 5.2). In earlier chapters, we saw that Early Horizon health, labor, diet, and biological kinship were not stratified by burial location or sex, perhaps suggesting that social hierarchy was limited or not reflected by burial location. Cranial modification adds to this picture as it also did not correlate with burial location or sex. Individuals from many demographic categories exhibited different styles of cranial modification (or lack thereof) and were not necessarily buried together nor isolated from other individuals. In fact,

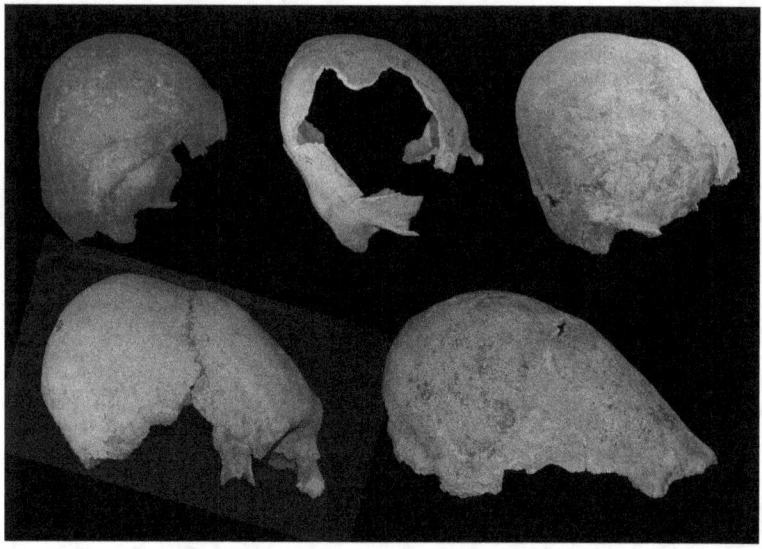

Figure 5.6 Examples of cranial modification from the Early Horizon. Top row: erect modification. Bottom row: oblique modification.

Figure 5.7 Example of skeletal trauma from the Early Horizon, a perimortem fracture of the frontal of a juvenile individual.

in one instance, a young adult with erect modification was buried with an unmodified subadult around 6–8 years old at the time of death. While we cannot confidently characterize the relationship between these individuals, the inclusion together in a tomb at least indicates that the same people were in charge of interring them, suggesting perhaps a familial or kin relationship. Clearly cranial modification did not limit contact between the modified and unmodified.

Perhaps the diversity in cranial modification style can be explained because of the migration from other regions, i.e., nonlocal individuals were bringing their foreign practices or their previously modified heads with them into the lake basin. Unfortunately, only two Early Horizon individuals were tested for strontium isotopes. One of these individuals was in fact nonlocal, but neither tested individual had observable crania for modification, making connections between biological kinship, geographic origins, and modification unclear. However, more broadly, biological kinship did not mark differences between the modified and unmodified, no matter their geographic origins. And no matter their origins, there was an overall lack of trauma during this period. Taking these lines of evidence together, it seems likely that cranial modification diversity during the Early Horizon did not lead to increased interpersonal violence, either because groups were not violently competitive, or modification style was not a significant indicator of competing groups.

Early Intermediate Period

Twenty-four individuals were observed for cranial modification; of these, six individuals (25%) displayed oblique modification while five showed (21%) erect modification (Table 5.1; Figures 5.2, 5.8). Thirteen individuals (54%) were unmodified. Individuals with oblique modification included two juveniles (one of indeterminate sex, one probable male), one probable female mature adult, and one probable female old adult. Individuals with erect modification included one juvenile, three male or probable male young adults, and one male adult.

Ten (17%) of 58 observable individuals experienced trauma (Table 5.1; Figure 5.4, 5.9). Five individuals experienced cranial trauma (Figures 5.9a, 5.9b) while another five individuals showed evidence of postcranial trauma (Figures 5.9c, 5.9d). Cranial trauma included four instances of parietal trauma on one male, two probable males, and one probable female adults, and one instance of frontal trauma on a male young adult. Three of four instances of cranial trauma were located at or above the "hat-brim" line, towards the crown of the head, suggesting interpersonal conflict as the cause. Two individuals with parietal trauma also underwent cranial surgery, or trepanation, associated with their fractures, indicating that some level of medical intervention was possible for those traumatized (Figures 5.9a, 5.9b). One individual survived this medical intervention, likely for years

78 *Growing Divisions: Violence and Identity*

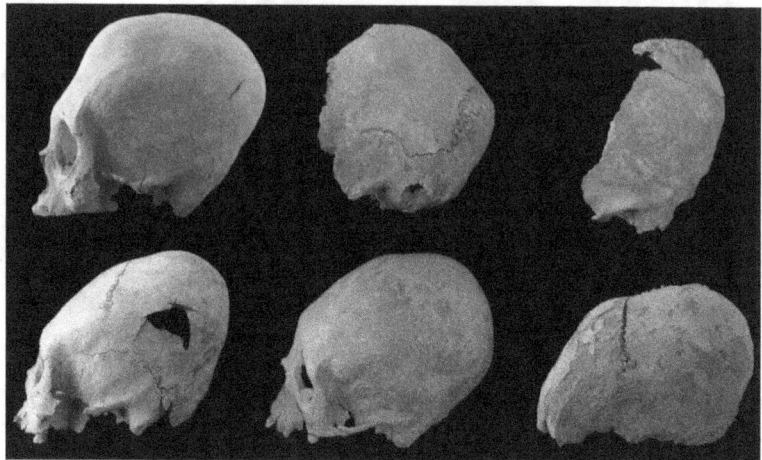

Figure 5.8 Examples of cranial modification from the EIP. Top row: erect modification. Bottom row: oblique modification.

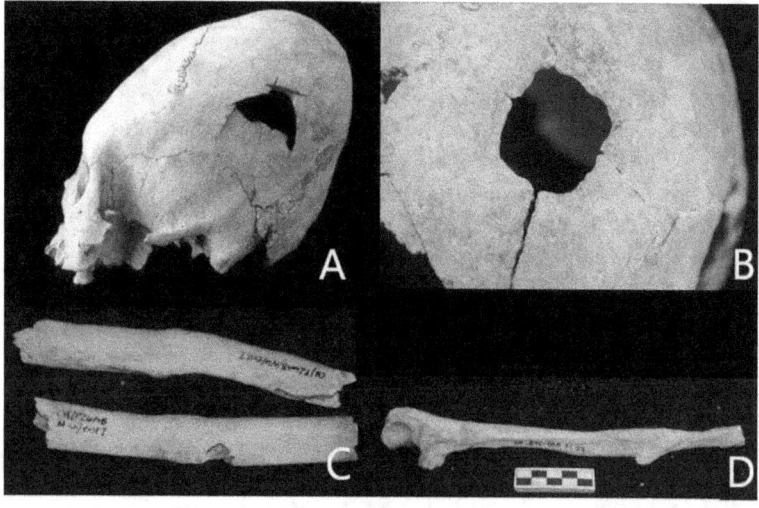

Figure 5.9 Examples of skeletal trauma from the EIP, including a perimortem cranial fracture and subsequent incomplete surgical intervention to remove piece of broken bone (A), an antemortem cranial fracture and healed subsequent surgical intervention (B), two healed rib fractures (C), and a healed ulnar fracture (D).

afterwards, allowing the fracture and subsequent surgical intervention to heal with rounded edges (Figure 5.9b) (Juengst and Chávez 2015). While likely originally stemming from a violent encounter, the successful treatment of this fracture suggests that trauma was also cured in the wake of its creation. Postcranial trauma included cutmarks on the posterior distal femur of a female adolescent, a healed distal ulnar fracture on a male young adult, a healed distal radial fracture on a probable female young adult and healed rib fractures on two female young adults.

There were some interesting connections between trauma and cranial modification during the EIP (Table 5.2). Three of six (50%) individuals with oblique modification (one probable male juvenile, one probable female young adult, and one probable female mature adult) were traumatized, exhibiting lesions consistent with perimortem cranial trauma and antemortem rib fractures. Three of five (60%) individuals with erect modification experienced trauma including two instances of antemortem cranial trauma and one instance of perimortem cranial trauma. Three of 13 (23%) unmodified individuals presented with trauma, including two fractures of the lower arm and one rib fracture.

The Early Intermediate Period individuals demonstrate a statistical connection between trauma and presence of cranial modification. Oblique, erect, and unmodified crania were present in this sample; however, individuals with modified crania were statistically more likely to experience skeletal trauma, while those with unmodified crania were traumatized less frequently. Additionally, half of the trauma was cranial, which is highly correlated with interpersonal violence. In contrast, traumatized individuals with unmodified crania exhibited no cranial trauma, and predominantly suffered lower arm and wrist fractures, an injury most often the result of falling on an outstretched hand (Walker 2001).

Thus, during the EIP, it seems having any type of cranial modification placed one at higher risk of interpersonal conflict resulting in cranial trauma. Perhaps these highly visible markers of identity did in fact become a liability, labeling modified individuals as outsiders and/or acceptable targets of violence. Alternatively, modified individuals could be injured outside of Copacabana communities; when venturing away from the lake basin, cranial modification may have made someone stand out in the wrong ways, whereas unmodified individuals could travel more incognito. Exploring these changes in context of the larger environmental changes may help clarify these issues.

Increasing Violence and Diversity over Time?

There are some interesting temporal changes in cranial modification. First, after the initial lack of obliquely modified and unmodified crania in the Preceramic, diversity in modification style increased during the Early Horizon and EIP. This could reflect the limited size of PC sample, or the fact that all the Preceramic burials stem from the same burial location, while the Early Horizon and EIP samples include several burial sites. Archaeologically, we suspect that the Copacabana Peninsula was fairly sparsely populated during the Preceramic as mobile groups ranged through the region in pursuit of wild game and prime fishing locations (Aldenderfer 1989; Stanish 2003). Perhaps for these smaller groups, quickly identifying group members by head shape was key to avoiding strangers and thus avoiding violent conflicts.

Within the later samples, multiple modification styles were identified at all burial locations, suggesting that more communities or lineages were present in the lake basin during the Early Horizon and EIP, perhaps living in multi-ethnic settlements (or at least, creating multi-ethnic burial grounds). However, despite an increase in modification styles, cranial modification did not become mandatory nor the norm, as the majority of individuals remained unmodified during the latter periods. It is possible modification was limited to certain special individuals, perhaps of elevated rank or elite lineage. However, a lack of modification does not vary consistently with markers of low status, such as a dearth of grave goods or poor health. And unmodified and modified individuals can be found sharing the same burial location, and in some cases, even the same tomb. Thus, it seems more likely that unmodified individuals did not undergo this process for reasons unrelated to status (although not necessarily all for the same reasons). Whether or not unmodified individuals represent a cohesive group, it is clear that people maintained a variety of approaches to cranial modification over time.

Violence and modification vary over time, but do not show significant links until the EIP. What changed between the Early Horizon and EIP that connected cranial modification with trauma risk? First, trauma dramatically increased overall during the EIP, a statistically significant change compared to other periods, not just for unmodified peoples. This marked development of violence could be related to several social and environmental trends: increased social ranking, increased sedentism and territoriality, and a prolonged period of drought, resulting in depleted lake resources (Bandy 2004; Capriles et al. 2016). Likely, these factors are interrelated; a prolonged drought likely encouraged investment in alternate terrestrial sources of food, wild and agricultural (Capriles et al. 2016; Juengst et al. 2021). If new subsistence strategies meant people competed for access to land, or access to resources more broadly, violence may have escalated as part of this competition.

Under the new environmental and economic regimes, cooperative behaviors from the Early Horizon may not have been promoted and people may have tightened group boundaries as competition increased (Barth 1969). Highly visible group identity markers, such as cranial modification, would have then increased risk of violence both at home and abroad. Within the lake basin, modified individuals may have become acceptable targets of corporal punishment, marked as different from the unmodified majority. If these individuals traveled abroad, they may have been conspicuous as foreigners with differently shaped heads. This double bind of at-home and foreign violence clearly resulted in elevated trauma for modified individuals.

However, even with this increased risk of violence, individuals with different styles of cranial modification were still buried at the same sites and individuals with modified heads received medical treatment for violent injuries. Thus, while cranial modification may have identified some as acceptable targets of violence, EIP society still allowed all to access the same sacred sites for burial and provided avenues for care-taking of the injured. It seems that the violence of the EIP was not extreme enough to exclude people entirely and may have worked as a stabilizer, maintaining community during uncertain environmental times.

6 Building Community
Navigating New Terrain

So how can bioarchaeologists combine these lines of evidence to think about power in the past? What can we learn from the Copacabana Peninsula that is applicable to other parts of the global past, or our modern lives? This chapter looks closely at each period and identifies trends in power and community in relationship to larger environmental and social changes. Finally, the chapter considers how to apply these ideas to other studies of the past and present.

The Preceramic Period

The Preceramic individuals were excavated from the same site, Muruqullu. Given the proximity of the burials to each other, the overall small sample, and the phenotypic similarities between the buried individuals, it is likely that this group represents one particular Preceramic community, perhaps burying their dead at this location for a generation or two. The skeletal indicators assessed here show that this group living on and around the Copacabana Peninsula organized society in interesting ways. On the one hand, low-level endemic disease was likely an issue for them, perhaps contracting nonfatal zoonotic diseases related to their regular interaction with and consumption of wild and domesticated camelids and lake fish. Preceramic peoples lead intense physical lives, resulting in the regular experience of osteoarthritis. However, no particular demographic group was at higher risk of disease or labor-related degeneration, nor limited in access to dietary resources, and people were generally closely related to one another. This combination of factors suggests that ranked social hierarchy was not present within this group during this time.

On the other hand, cranial modification and trauma indicate that competition between groups might have been common. All observable individuals displayed erect cranial modification, and two modified

DOI: 10.4324/9781003175971-6

individuals suffered trauma, with a third individual traumatized and unobservable for cranial trauma. It seems possible that having a highly visible and permanent identity marker (like a modified cranium) created important group boundaries and elevated risk of violence during this time. Given that these particular individuals appear to have had equal access to resources and similar experiences of disease, it seems that the violence likely stemmed from outside the group. While cranial modification heightened group cohesion and resource-sharing *within* the group, modification may have made interacting with people from other groups more fraught.

Cranial modification has been reported from other Preceramic burials around the lake basin as well (Haas and Viviano Llave 2015). Burials from the western side of the lake, in modern day Peru, displayed both erect and oblique modification and also had evidence of violent skeletal trauma. While both types of modification were present at this burial site, Haas and Viviano Llave (2015) argued that the cranial modification in conjunction with the evidence for projectile and blunt force trauma in their sample, evidenced the development of local competitive groups in the western lake basin.

Local intergroup competition with in-group cooperation seems like the clearest explanation for the combination of skeletal factors seen in the Preceramic individuals. Preceramic peoples likely cooperated in order to hunt, herd, and fish, shared resources with family and group members, and worked together to survive zoonotic diseases and traumatic injury. They marked their identities in highly visible ways, which promoted in-group cohesion and belonging. However, in the challenging landscape of the Titicaca Basin, they likely had to compete with other people to control territory and other resources. Thus, cooperation and competition were both important parts of Preceramic social organization and community.

The Early Horizon

During the Early Horizon, people were buried at a number of different sites across the Copacabana Peninsula, including Ch'isi, Muruqullu, Cundisa, and Kenasfena. All associated with Yaya-Mama temples, these interments varied from place to place and tomb to tomb in terms of types of grave goods and style of burial, but no pattern of status is identifiable based on mortuary aspects alone. Skeletal evidence suggests that perhaps cooperation, anarchy, and/or heterarchy may be good models of power for the social organization of the Early Horizon. This is visible through several patterns. First, although lesions associated with malnutrition and stress increased in frequency from Preceramic rates, these markers were not clustered more heavily on particular demographic groups or at specific burial sites. Bodily stress seemed to be an issue that the whole population struggled with and was likely linked to the inclusion of new dietary resources, and more importantly, the risks associated with sedentary settlements and zoonotic disease. Second, special foods such as maize were not hoarded or exploited only by particular individuals in society but were also at least occasionally available to most. Additionally, biological kinship and labor did not mark differences between individuals, including those with diverse styles of cranial modification and one individual who was from a different part of the Andes. Finally, rates of skeletal trauma were significantly lower than during other periods, with only a single individual suffering a skeletal fracture.

None of the various aspects of life that these lines of evidence reflect (disease, labor, food, family, identity, and violence) were organized hierarchically or in ways that limited access or increased risk for particular groups of individuals. Rather than hoarding or competing for resources, people seem to have shared resources and workloads, experienced similar rates and types of illness, and lived nonviolently in communities composed of people from various ethnic or identity groups. Power may have been shared, with groups cooperating to provide the labor required to cultivate fields, build terraces, and maintain trade networks (Chávez, K. and Chávez, S. 1997; S. Chávez 2012:449; DeMarrais 2016). Ancestry and kinship may have been integral to this process, alongside ritual participation.

The emergence of the Yaya-Mama Religious Tradition during this time is significant, as these temple complexes would have necessitated significant coordinated labor to construct (Chávez 2012). However, rather than mandating top-down ranked power to motivate this labor, the religious tradition may have actually helped promote cooperative labor. Temple activities could have reinforced kinship relationships, both biological and symbolic, through burial of the dead and ancestor veneration. Yaya-Mama iconography emphasizing duality of males and female individuals and reproduction in nature, combined with the open nature of the temples and burial of young individuals at key locations, suggests that ancestor veneration was likely central to Yaya-Mama ritual (Hastorf 2003; Juengst 2018) and making biological and symbolic kinship central to community.

The inclusion of numerous juvenile burials suggests that kinship and lineages played a role in labor sharing during the Early Horizon and into the EIP. In the Andes more broadly, deceased children and infants were often buried at places significant to community identity (Allen 2012; Baitzel 2018; Blom and Knudson 2020; Toyne 2018; van Kessel 2001), a persistent trend that Catholic priests attempted to take advantage of, replacing local ancestor cults with Christianity by including children in church burials (Wernke 2007). In the modern day, Bolivian indigenous Aymara peoples celebrate infants (wawas) and children at naming ceremonies and/or when they receive their first haircut and are considered to be officially members of the family and society (Allen 2012; Blom and Couture 2018). While the antiquity of this practice is unknown, the emphasis on the importance of young children and family lineages remains today. Perhaps the high proportion of infant and juvenile burials buried at Yaya-Mama temples during the Early Horizon and into the EIP suggests a similar importance, linking children, ancestors, and community. Burying young individuals at ritually significant centers linked them to their ancestral lineage, simultaneously creating these young dead as symbolic ancestors for individual lineages while also reinforcing ties to community lineages more broadly.

Yaya-Mama also could have mitigated social tensions through ritual sharing of *chicha* (maize beer), a drink which served to bond and strengthen relationships between sharers. Chicha has played many roles in the Andes over time, often demarcating social class and power relationships based on access to this important substance (Bray 2009; Goldstein 2003; Goldstein et al. 2009; Logan et al. 2012). In some larger, corporate settings (i.e., feasts hosted by the Inka Empire) chicha was used to increase hierarchy and emphasize difference through selective access (Bray 2009). However, here, the shared increase in C_4 consumption during the Early Horizon suggests that most had access to maize in small amounts. Logan et al. (2012) suggest that sharing chicha at temples during the Early Horizon and EIP on the southern Taraco Peninsula in the southern Titicaca Basin was central to Yaya-Mama ceremonies of ancestor veneration, based on analysis of *keros* and shared public architecture. Those ceremonies likely also worked to reinforce community bonds, through the sharing of that beverage (Janusek 2008; Logan et al. 2012). Interestingly, fermentation of maize sugar may result in less positive C_4 values, compared to unfermented maize (Canal 2006:30). Thus, drinking fermented C_4 resources (as compared to eating C_4 resources directly) may have a weakened impact on C_4 signatures. The slight positive change in C_4 values during the Early Horizon may be the result of drinking chicha, especially given the connection with burial at temple sites. Imbibing ritual drink at Yaya-Mama ceremonies may have been an important mechanism for creating and maintaining community.

Finally, the ritual institution could have redistributed resources including food and marshalled the labor necessary to support the emerging agricultural and sedentary settlements. Because sedentary settlements, civic architecture, and agricultural fields often require more physical labor than mobile housing and foraging for resources, archaeologists have at times assumed that these chores required coercion and top-down control to convince people to perform them (Earle 1997; Kolata 1993; Service 1962; Stanish 2003, 2004; Webster 1990). However, increasing evidence from modern and prehistoric peoples demonstrate that intensive agricultural and complex building tasks, such as raised field agriculture and the agricultural terraces built around the Copacabana Peninsula, can be achieved through familial and local community-based efforts (DeMarrais 2016; Erickson 1993, 1996, 2006; Erickson and Candler 1989; Kolb 1997; Kolb and Snead 1997). The skeletal evidence here demonstrates that people accessed food and experienced health relatively equitably and that physical labor actually did not increase in ways that impacted the skeleton throughout the Early Horizon. Labor related to terrace and temple construction, food acquisition, and other daily chores must have been shared rather than loaded upon the shoulders of a few. While impressive and complex, the terraces and other agricultural investments of the period likely have resulted from consensus and communal labor, rather than coerced or competitive relationships.

It seems very likely that during the Early Horizon, ritual and kinship enabled and maintained cooperative relationships to achieve common tasks, rather than hierarchical or competitive systems of power. This local community-centered social organization does not mean that perfect equality existed, nor that conflict was entirely absent. Rather, what the evidence from this period shows is that cooperation in achieving tasks made it possible for many people to access adequate resources and mitigated extreme violence or targeting of certain individuals, even when expressing different social identities or coming from diverse areas of the Andes.

The Early Intermediate Period

During the Early Intermediate Period, people living on the Copacabana Peninsula encountered different social circumstances. Rates of pathological stress lesions did not increase overall; however, certain groups (namely females and probable females) more often presented these lesions compared to females in earlier periods and to other adults during the EIP. Diets shifted towards terrestrial resources, particularly concerning types of protein, although in general, people were eating similar resources and laboring similar amounts (and less intensely when compared to earlier periods). People were still closely related overall, but often grew up in different parts of the Andes and displayed a variety of types of cranial modification. Most dramatically, violent trauma was experienced much more frequently during this period, particularly as reflected on the skeletons of females and probable females.

Many factors likely prompted these changes, including environmental circumstances that may have led to more competition and increased regional violence. There were several periods of drought during the Early Horizon and Early Intermediate Period, one of which reached its lowest point around AD 100. Lake levels did not rebound from this for several hundred years, encompassing the entire EIP (Abbott et al. 1997; Baker et al. 2005; Weide et al. 2017). This drought could have limited resource availability in a few ways: (1) lake resources may have been more limited, as shores constricted and aquatic species become scarcer or harder to capture; and (2) investment in terrestrial resources might increase territoriality, as field and pasture space became more important commodities (Bandy 2004). If drought or lower-lake levels complicated resources acquisition, incipient agriculture and land negotiations, the resultant competition for resources may have led to ranked social inequality and group circumscription.

Alternatively (or additionally), social organization and violence in other areas of the lake basin many have influenced events in the southern lake basin. Beginning in the Early Horizon around 500 BC, emergent ritual in the northern lake basin appeared to venerate individuals and military prowess, unlike Yaya-Mama iconography seen in the southern lake basin. Northern sites were built in more defensible locations, and excavations at the Pukara temple produced several trophy heads, perhaps taken in battle (Arkush 2008; Stanish and Levine 2011). By the first century AD, evidence for escalating violence and warfare dramatically culminated with the razing of Taraco, an important ceremonial site (Levine 2012; Stanish and Levine 2011). This conflict in the north could have spread throughout the lake basin over time. If people living on the Copacabana Peninsula became increasingly concerned about violent northern neighbors, they may have reacted by creating stricter group boundaries and territories.

Looking at the Andes more broadly, the EIP was a time when many people experienced increased violence (Arkush and Tung, 2013). In the first "horizon" of warfare, people across the Andes experienced an increase in violence that resulted in skeletal trauma, built more defensive architecture, and created iconography depicting warriors and warfare. While there was some local variability in the extent of violent expression, this pan-Andean upswing in violence does not seem to be correlated with a pan-Andean change in the climate. Rather than associated with environmental change or adoption of agriculture, Arkush and Tung argue, "(i)ntense warfare, instead, arose in a context of emerging social stratification and elite rivalry, made fluid by the failure of the preexisting authority system" (2013:326).

While social stratification and violence may have been emerging around the Andes during the EIP, society on the Copacabana Peninsula seems a little more complicated. On the one hand, females and probably females seem to have suffered disproportionately during this time, with significantly more trauma and lesions associated with stress and disease, and cranial modification made some a target for violence, compared to those with unmodified crania. On the other hand, these identity markers (biological sex and body modification) did not preclude burial at certain sites, change access to food, nor limit biological relationships. While the cooperative and anarchical relationships of the Early Horizon appear to have disappeared during this time, it is not clear that purely competitive ranked social hierarchy replaced them.

Perhaps more heterarchical and fluid power relationships may be an appropriate interpretation for EIP social organization. People may have deployed competitive power at key moments for access to territory or when confronting someone from a different region, resulting in elevated violence against those with identifiable cultural markers. The strategic and situational use of power was perhaps more strongly associated with male social roles, resulting in high rates of trauma and nutritional insults among females. However, there was not an accepted top-down system of hierarchy that meant some people were always considered lower-class in all social circumstances. These gendered and situational power dynamics seem consistent with heterarchy over strict ranked social hierarchy.

Heterarchy of labor and kinship has been well documented in the lake basin during later time periods, under the Tiwanaku state (AD 400–1100). Tiwanaku was an influential state that colonized several areas of the Andes, with its social and ritual capital (also called Tiwanaku) in the southern lake basin. Labor organization under Tiwanaku was likely heterarchical, with different groups performing different tasks for the state and their livelihoods (Becker 2016, 2017; Janusek 2008). At the core site of Tiwanaku, ethnic neighborhoods devoted to different craft or economic production have been identified, based on the presence of different artifact types (Janusek 2008). Becker (2017) supported this interpretation by showing that muscle markers related to repetitive labor also differed for these groups, indicating that they were engaging in different daily activities. In fact, Becker noted that at several Tiwanaku sites, males and females appeared to have habitually performed different tasks. While skeletal markers of labor did not yet indicate sex differences in this study, Perhaps this tradition of labor divisions between sexes and local groups developed during the EIP in the southern lake basin.

The Impact Of Environmental And Social Changes

Overall, it is clear that no single type of power or social organization persisted on the Copacabana Peninsula, but people deployed cooperative and competitive strategies at various times. A number of variables affected what types of social organization were successful, and it is likely that these societies were never entirely equal nor entirely competitive. Rather, people made decisions about power and social relationships based on a variety of factors, including environment, social institutions, and regional trends.

Many studies of climate change and impacts on human interactions have suggested that resource scarcity can lead to social inequality and increased violence (i.e., Allen et al. 2016; Carneiro 1970; Harrod and Martin 2014; Redfern 2020) and it is clear that at times that was true for the Copacabana Peninsula. Environmental fluctuations in precipitation caused lake level changes that altered social roles and relationships, increasing violence and competition in certain spheres of EIP daily life. In particular, low lake levels during the EIP escalated violence for females, perhaps related to changing gender roles or other aspects of what it meant to be biologically female for these peoples. Those with cranial modification were also at higher risk of trauma, no matter which type of modification was performed, suggesting that being visibly identifiable as belonging to a certain group elevated risk of violence. However, the climatic shift did not necessitate clear or uniform hierarchy for all people. While the evidence for increasing trauma and disease load for some suggests that in certain aspects of life, inequality increased, other measures of inequality such as limited mobility or biological or ethnic exclusion remain unchanged from earlier periods. Environmental change may have prompted increased competition and inequality in some aspects of Copacabana life, but the new power structures and social relationships were not clearly hierarchical or uniform.

The social environment of the Copacabana Peninsula also played an important role in determining power dynamics, at times mitigating inequality and changing the nature of social interactions. For example, not every decrease in lake level was associated with increased violence. One of the lowest lake levels occurred around 400 BC when the data do not reflect increased social inequality, trauma, or resource hoarding. During the Early Horizon, the Yaya-Mama Religious Tradition seems to have focused on ancestor veneration and community-building as demonstrated by the architecture, ceremonial activities, and iconography associated with the temples (Chávez 2004; 2012; Hastorf 2003). Skeletal evidence from the time also indicates a lack of clear hierarchy and shows that people had similar risks of disease, malnutrition and violence, labored cooperatively, and were not excluded from movement and family. While many factors likely contributed to this trend, the Yaya-Mama focus on community-building mitigated competition and hierarchical systems of power, instead encouraging cooperation to construct temples and terraces, share resources, and interact with people coming from distant lands. The changes to environment were thus less impactful; the community emphasized by Yaya-Mama was able to help navigate lake level changes and the presumed resource scarcity in ways that limited violent competition.

Overall, it is clear that community and power in the Titicaca Basin during the Preceramic, Early Horizon, and EIP were not dictated by any one person or group, or required to conform to any particular form or structure. People navigated the physical environment by creating social structures that supported them and allowed them to successfully live in a challenging landscape. They employed different responses in the face of climate change, creating social institutions to help navigate challenges during one period and potentially tightening community boundaries when drought coincided with regional violence. And at all times, individuals experienced care, created families, and shared food with each other, most often cooperating to achieve their daily tasks and find their way through daily life.

Broader Implications And Future Research

The fact that the social systems can mitigate the impacts of environmental change is clearly relevant to other societies around the world in the past and present. While local environments and reliability of resource acquisition play central roles to human societies, humans are masterful in their ability to modify environments and create cultural structures that mitigate, expand, and alter the possibilities offered by nature. Archaeologists should not assume that resource scarcity was always a motivator for violence, or that competition was the only viable reaction to changes in resource availability. Additionally, human innovation and creativity in modifying the environment and in reacting to environmental changes should be encouraging for the future as humans navigate new challenges on a global scale. Approaches to broad-scale shifts to the climate can be navigated through consensus and cooperation, rather than necessitating increased inequality and competition. This may however require a shared focus on community rather than placing emphasis on individuals or specific lineages.

Understanding that cooperation and anarchy are viable routes towards complex social organization are important lessons over time and space. Often, archaeologists and other social theorists are hampered by their own experiences of social organization and at times, may even be searching for a justification for their own society's ideologies and empirical expansions (Borck 2019; Borck and Clark 2021). The idea that complexity necessitates hierarchy and competition is deeply rooted in Western thought, evidenced by Charles Darwin's early embrace of competition as the natural mode of evolution (Darwin 1999 [1839]) and the foundational investigations of Classical Greek competitive states (Winkelmann 1850). This has resulted in an enduring assumption that competition and inequality are primary motivators for social changes and developments among human societies (i.e., Morgan 1877; Service 1962; Tylor 2006 [1861]). Archaeologists should bear in mind that coercive hierarchy is not necessary for complicated labor tasks, religious systems, or agricultural success. Cooperation and consensus may have been just as common, if not more frequent, than competition and coercion. And importantly, these processes are neither teleological nor unchangeable once established. For instance, on the Copacabana Peninsula, competitive foraging groups were succeeded by collaborative semi-agricultural communities who were followed by agricultural groups practicing a mix of power strategies during an uncertain time. Social organizations are created by people and through actions, and communities are not fixed in destiny to be one type or another.

Archaeologists are increasingly asking when and why did cooperative relationships emerge, rather than investigating the origins of social inequality (i.e., Graber and Wengrow 2021). This is an important disciplinary shift as "pre-figuring" a past that is biased towards inequality may in fact lead to or justify the inequality present today (Borck 2018). Future archaeological research should continue this track and investigate not just the origins of social inequality but also ask about nuances to power. Why do some deploy cooperative strategies while others compete and vice versa? When and why do people use mixed strategies? In doing so, archaeologists can produce a more complete picture of the human past and contribute to a growing understanding of what it means to be human in the modern world.

References

Abbott, M. B., Binford, M. W., Brenner, M., & Kelts, K. R. (1997). A 350014C yr high-resolution record of water-level changes in Lake Titicaca, Bolivia/Peru. *Quaternary Research* 47(2): 169–180. doi:10.1006/qres.1997.1881

Abercrombie, T. A. (1998). *Pathways of Memory and Power: Ethnography and History among an Andean People*. University of Wisconsin Press: Madison.

Acsadi, G., & Nemeskéri, J. (1970). *History of Human Life Span and Mortality*. Translated by K. Balas. Akadémiai Kiadó: Budapest.

Aldenderfer, M. S. (1989). The Archaic Period in the south-central Andes. *Journal of World Prehistory* 3(2): 117–158.

Aldenderfer M. S. (2010). Gimme That Old Time Religion: Rethinking the role of religion in the emergence of social inequality. In: Price T. D., Feinman G. M. (Eds.) *Pathways to Power. Fundamental Issues in Archaeology*, pp. 77–94. Springer: New York, NY. doi:10.1007/978-1-4419-6300-0_4

Allen, C. J. (2012). *The Hold Life Has: Coca and Cultural Identity in an Andean Community*, 2nd edition. Smithsonian Institution: Washington DC.

Allen, M. W., Bettinger, R. L., Codding, B. F., Jones, T. L., & Schwitalla, A. W. (2016). Resource scarcity drives lethal aggression among prehistoric hunter-gatherers in central California. *Proceedings of the National Academy of Sciences*, 113(43), 12120–12125.

Allison, M. J., Gerszten, E., Munizaga, J., Santoro, C., & Focacci, G. (1981). La práctica de la deformación craneana entre los pueblos andinos precolombinos. *Chungara: Revista de Antropología Chilena* 7: 238–260.

Ambrose, S. H. (1993). Isotopic Analysis: Methodological and Interpretive Considerations. In: Sanford M. K. (Ed.) *Investigations of Ancient Human Tissues: Chemical Analysis in Anthropology*, pp. 59–130. Gordon and Breach: Amsterdam.

Ambrose, S. H., & Norr, L. (1993). Experimental evidence for the relationship of the carbon isotope ratios of whole diet and dietary protein to those of bone collagen and carbonate. In Lambert J. B., Grupe G. (Eds.) *Prehistoric human bone*, pp. 1–37. Springer, Berlin, Heidelberg. doi: 10.1007/978-3-662-02894-0_1

Anderson, B. R. (1983). *Imagined Communities: Reflections on the Origina and Spread of Nationalism*. Verso: London.

Andrushko, V. A., Pino, E. C. T., & Bellifemine, V. (2006). The Burials at Sacsahuaman and Chokepukio: A bioarchaeological case study of imperialism from the capital of the Inca Empire. *Ñawpa Pacha* 28(1), 63–92. doi:10.1179/naw.2006.28.1.005

Angelbeck, B. (2016). The balance of autonomy and alliance in anarchic societies: the organization of defences in the Coast Salish past. *World Archaeology* 48(1):51–69. https://doi.org/10.1080/00438243.2015.1131620

Angelbeck B. & C. Grier. (2012) Anarchism and the archaeology of anarchic societies. *Current Anthropology* 53(4):547–587. doi:10.1086/667621

Angelbeck, B. Borck, L. & Sanger, M. (2018). Anarchist theory and archaeology. In: Smith C. (Ed.) *Encyclopedia of Global Archaeology*, pp. 1–8. Springer Nature: Switzerland. doi:10.1007/978-3-319-51726-1_2627-1

Appadurai, A. (1988). Putting hierarchy in its place. *Cultural Anthropology* 3 (1): 36–49.

Araújo, A., Reinhard, K., Leles, D., Sianto, L., Iñiguez, A., Fugassa, M, Arriaza, B., Orellana, N., & Fernando Ferreira, L. (2011). Paleoepidemiology of intestinal parasites and lice in Pre-Columbian South America. *Chungara: Revista de Antropología Chilena* 43(2): 303–13.

Arkush, E. (2008). War, chronology, and causality in the Titicaca Basin. *Latin American Antiquity* 19(4), 339–373.

Arkush, E. & Allen, M. W. (2006). *The Archaeology of Warfare: Prehistories of Raiding And Conquest*. University Press of Florida: Gainesville.

Arkush, E., & Tung, T. A. (2013). Patterns of war in the Andes from the Archaic to the Late Horizon: insights from settlement patterns and cranial trauma. *Journal of Archaeological Research* 21(4): 307–369. doi:10.1007/s10814-013-9065-1

Armelagos, G. J., Goodman, A. H., Harper, K. N., & Blakey, M. L. (2009). Enamel hypoplasia and early mortality: Bioarcheological support for the Barker hypothesis. *Evolutionary Anthropology* 18(6): 261–271. doi:10.1002/evan.20239

Arnold, D. Y., & Hastorf, C. A. (2008). *Heads of State: Icons, Power, and Politics in the Ancient and Modern Andes*. Left Coast Press: Berkeley.

Atkinson, M. (2002). *Tattooed: The Sociogenesis of a Body Art*. University of Toronto Press: Toronto, ON.

Aufderheide, A. C., Rodríguez-Martín, C., & Langsjoen, O. (1998). *The Cambridge Encyclopedia of Human Paleopathology*. Cambridge University Press: Cambridge.

Baitzel, S. (2018). Parental grief and mourning in the ancient Andes. *Journal of Archaeological Method and Theory* 25(1): 178–201. doi:10.1007/s10816-017-9333-3

Baker, P. A., Fritz, S. C., Garland, J., & Ekdahl, E. (2005). Holocene hydrologic variation at Lake Titicaca, Bolivia/Peru, and its relationship to North Atlantic climate variation. *Journal of Quaternary Science* 20(7–8): 655–662. doi:10.1002/jqs.987.

Bandy, M. S. (2004). Fissioning, scalar stress, and social evolution in early village societies. *American Anthropologist* 106(2): 322–333. doi:10.1525/aa.2004.106.2.322

Barth, F. (1969). *Ethnic Groups and Boundaries: The Social Organisation of Culture Difference.* Allen & Unwin: London.

Baucom, P. C., & Rigsby, C. A. (1999). Climate and lake-level history of the northern Altiplano, Bolivia, as recorded in Holocene sediments of the Rio Desaguadero. *Journal of Sedimentary Research* 69(3): 597–611.

Becker, S. K. (2016). Skeletal evidence of craft production from the Ch'iji Jawira site in Tiwanaku, Bolivia. *Journal of Archaeological Science: Reports* 9: 405–415. doi:10.1016/j.jasrep.2016.08.017

Becker, S. K. (2017). Community labor and laboring communities within the Tiwanaku state (CE 500–1100). *Archeological Papers of the American Anthropological Association* 28(1): 38–53. doi:10.1111/apaa.12087

Becker, S. K. (2020). Osteoarthritis, entheses, and long bone cross-sectional geometry in the Andes: Usage, history, and future directions. *International Journal of Paleopathology* 29: 45–53. doi:10.1016/j.ijpp.2019.08.005

Berger, E., Yang, L., & Ye, W. (2019). Foot binding in a Ming dynasty cemetery near Xi'an, China. *International Journal of Paleopathology* 24: 79–88. doi:10.1016/j.ijpp.2018.09.005

Berryman, C. A. (2010). *Food, feasts, and the construction of identity and power in ancient Tiwanaku: a bioarchaeological perspective.* (Order No. 3445644). [Doctoral dissertation, Vanderbilt University]. ProQuest Dissertations & Theses Global. www.proquest.com/dissertations-theses/food-feasts-construction-identity-power-ancient/docview/854982978/se-2?accountid=14605

Berryman, H. E., & Haun, S. J. (1996). Applying forensic techniques to interpret cranial fracture patterns in an archaeological specimen. *International Journal of Osteoarchaeology* 6(1): 2–9. doi:10.1002/(SICI)1099-1212(199601)6:1<2::AID-OA244>3.0.CO;2-R

Blackmore, C. (2011). How to Queer the Past Without Sex: Queer theory, feminisms and the archaeology of identity. *Archaeologies* 7: 75–96. doi:10.1007/s11759-011-9157-9

Blom, D. E. (2005a). Embodying borders: human body modification and diversity in Tiwanaku society. *Journal of Anthropological Archaeology* 24(1): 1–24. doi:10.1016/j.jaa.2004.10.001

Blom, D. E. (2005b). A Bioarchaeological Approach to Tiwanaku Group Dynamics. In: Reycraft, R. (Ed.) *Us and Them: Archaeology and Ethnicity in the Andes*, pp. 153–182. Cotsen Institute of Archaeology, University of California: Los Angeles, CA.

Blom, D. E. & Couture, N. C. (2018). From wawa to "trophy head": Meaning, representation, and bioarchaeology of human heads from Ancient Tiwanaku. In: Tiesler, V. & Lozada, M. C. (Eds.) *Social Skins of the Head: Body Beliefs and Ritual in Ancient Mesoamerica and the Andes*, pp. 205–221. University of New Mexico Press: Albuquerque, NM.

Blom, D. E., & Knudson, K. J. (2020). Paleopathology and children in the Andes: Local/situated biologies and future directions. *International Journal of Paleopathology* 29: 65–75. doi:10.1016/j.ijpp.2019.08.004

Blom, D. E., Buikstra, J. E., Keng, L., Tomczak, P. D., Shoreman, E., & Stevens-Tuttle, D. (2005). Anemia and childhood mortality: Latitudinal patterning along the coast of pre-Columbian Peru. *American Journal of Physical Anthropology* 127(2): 152–169. doi:10.1002/ajpa.10431

Borck, L. (2018). Constructing the future history: prefiguration as historical epistemology and the chronopolitics of archaeology. *Journal of Contemporary Archaeology* 5(2): 213–302.

Borck, L. (2019). Constructing the future history: Prefiguration as historical epistemology and the chronopolitics of archaeology. *Journal of Contemporary Archaeology* 5(2): 229–238. doi:10.1558/jca.33560

Borck, L., & Clark, J. J. (2021). Dispersing Power: The Contentious, Egalitarian Politics of the Salado Phenomenon in the Hohokam Region of the U.S. Southwest. In: Thurston, T.L. & Fernández-Gotz, M. (Eds.), *Power from Below in Premodern Societies: The Dynamics of Political Complexity in the Archaeological Record*, pp. 247–271. Cambridge University Press: Cambridge.

Borck, L. S., & Sanger, M. C. (2017). An introduction to anarchism in archaeology. *SAA Archaeological Record* 17(1): 9–16. https://hdl.handle.net/1887/67984

Bourdieu, P. (1977). *Outline of a Theory of Practice*. Cambridge University Press: New York, NY.

Bray, T. (2009). The role of chicha in Inca State expansion: a distributional analysis of Inca aribalos. In Jennings, J. & Bowser, B.J. (Eds.), *Drink, Power, and Society in the Andes*, pp.108–132. Gainesville: University Press of Florida.

Bray, T. L. (Ed.). (2015). *The Archaeology of Wak'as: Explorations of the sacred in the pre-Columbian Andes*. University Press of Colorado: Denver.

Brickley, M. (2006). Rib fractures in the archaeological record: a useful source of sociocultural information?. *International Journal of Osteoarchaeology* 16(1): 61–75. doi:10.1002/oa.809

Brickley, M. & Ives, R. (2006). Skeletal manifestations of infantile scurvy. *American Journal of Physical Anthropology* 129(2): 163–172. doi:10.1002/ajpa.20265

Bridges, P. S. (1991). Degenerative joint disease in hunter–gatherers and agriculturalists from the southeastern United States. *American Journal of Physical Anthropology* 85(4): 379–391. doi:10.1002/ajpa.1330850403

Bridges, P. S. (1992). Prehistoric arthritis in the Americas. *Annual Review of Anthropology* 21(1): 67–91. doi:10.1146/annurev.an.21.100192.000435

Bridges, P. S. (1994). Vertebral arthritis and physical activities in the prehistoric Southeastern United States. *American Journal of Physical Anthropology* 93: 83–93. doi:10.1002/ajpa.1330930106

References

Brooks, S. T. & Suchey, J. M. (1990). Skeletal age determination based on the Os Pubis: A comparison of the Acsadi-Nemeskeri and Suchey-Brooks methods. *Human Evolution* 5: 227–238. doi:10.1007/BF02437238

Bruno, M. C. & Whitehead, W. T. (2003). Chenopodium Cultivation and Formative Period Agriculture at Chiripa, Bolivia. *Latin American Antiquity* 14(3): 339–355. doi:10.2307/3557565

Buikstra, J. E. & Meilke, J. H. (1985). Demography, diet, and health. In: Gilbert, Jr., R. I. & Meilke, J. H. (Eds.) *The Analysis of Prehistoric Diets*, pp. 359–422. Academic Press: New York, NY.

Buikstra, J. E. & Ubelaker, D.H. (Eds.) (1994). *Standards for Data Collection from Human Skeletal Remains*. Arkansas Archaeological Survey Research Series, 44. Arkansas Archeological Survey: Fayetteville.

Burger, R. L., Chávez, K. L. M., & Chávez, S. J. (2000). Through the Glass Darkly: Prehispanic obsidian procurement and exchange in Southern Peru and Northern Bolivia. *Journal of World Prehistory Journal of World Prehistory* 14(3), 267–362. doi:10.1023/A:1026509726643

Buzon, M. R., & Richman, R. (2007). Traumatic injuries and imperialism: The effects of Egyptian colonial strategies at Tombos in upper Nubia. *American Journal of Physical Anthropology* 133(2): 783–791. doi:10.1002/ajpa.20585

Canal, M. C. (2006). Stable Isotope Analysis and Maize-Stalk Beer Diet in Rats: Implications for the Origins of Maize. Master's Thesis, Department of Anthropology, University of British Columbia, Vancouver BC.

Canuto, M. A. & Yaeger, J. (Eds.) (2000). *Archaeology of Communities: A New World Perspective*. Routledge: New York, NY.

Capriles, J. M., Moore, K. M., Domic, A. I., & Hastorf, C. A. (2014). Fishing and environmental change during the emergence of social complexity in the Lake Titicaca Basin. *Journal of Anthropological Archaeology* 34: 66–77. doi:10.1016/j.jaa.2014.02.001

Capriles, J.M., Domic, A. I. & Moore, K. M. (2008). Fish remains from the Formative Period (1000 BC–AD 400) of Lake Titicaca, Bolivia: Zooarchaeology and taphonomy. *Quaternary International* 180: 115–126. doi:10.1016/j.quaint.2007.08.022

Capriles, J. M., Santoro, C. M., & Dillehay, T. D. (2016). Harsh environments and the terminal Pleistocene peopling of the Andean highlands. *Current Anthropology* 57(1): 99–100. doi:10.1086/684694

Carneiro, R. L. (1970). A theory of the origin of the state: Traditional theories of state origins are considered and rejected in favor of a new ecological hypothesis. *Science* 169(3947): 733–738.

Chávez, K. L. M. (1988). The significance of Chiripa in Lake Titicaca Basin developments. *Expedition* 30(3): 17–26.

Chávez, K. L. M. (1992.) The organization of production and distribution of traditional pottery in south highland Peru. In: Bey III, G. & Pool, C. (Eds.) *Ceramic Production and Distribution: An Integrated Approach*, pp. 49–92. Westview Books: Boulder.

References

Chávez, K. L. M., & Chávez, S. J. (1997). Current Research: The Yaya-Mama Archaeological Report, Copacabana, Bolivia. *Willay*, 44, 5–7.

Chávez, S. J. (1992). The conventionalized rules in Pukara pottery technology and iconography: implications for socio-political developments in the northern Lake Titicaca Basin. (Order No. 9314654) [Doctoral Dissertation, Michigan State University]. ProQuest Dissertations & Theses Global. www.proquest.com/dissertations-theses/conventionalized-rules-pucara-pottery-technology/docview/303972412/se-2?accountid=14605

Chávez, S. J. (2002). Identification of the camelid woman and feline man themes, motifs, and designs in Pucara style pottery. In: Silverman, H. & Isbell, W.H. (Eds.) *Andean Archaeology II; Art, Landscape, and Society*, pp. 35–69. Kluger Academic/Plenum Publishers: New York, NY.

Chávez, S. J. (2004). The Yaya-Mama Religious Tradition as an antecedent of Tiwanaku. In: Young-Sanchez, M. (Ed.) *Tiwanaku: Ancestors of the Inca*, pp. 70–75, 81–85, 88–93. Denver Art Institute and University of Nebraska Press: Lincoln, NE.

Chávez, S. J. (2008a). Integrating local communities in an archaeological project: experiments and prospects in Bolivia. In: McManamon, F. P., Stout, A., & Barnes, J. A. (Eds.) *Managing Archaeological Resources: Global Context, National Programs, and Local Actions*, pp. 257–275. Left Coast Press: Berkeley.

Chávez, S. J. (2008b). Resumen de los trabajos Arqueologicos del Proyecto Yaya-Mama en el sitio de Cundisa, Copacabana. *Chachapuma, December*.

Chávez, S. J. (2012). Agricultural terraces as monumental architecture in the Titicaca Basin. In: Burger, R. L. & Rosenswig, R. M. (Eds.) *Early New World Monumentality*, pp. 431–453. University of Florida Press: Gainesville, FL.

Chávez, S. J. & Chávez, K. L. M. (1970). Newly discovered monoliths from the highlands of Puno, Peru. *Expedition* 12(4): 25–39.

Chávez, S. J. & Chávez, K. L. M. (1976). A carved stela from Taraco, Puno, Peru, and the definition of an early style of stone sculpture from the altiplano of Peru and Bolivia. *Ñawpa Pacha* 13(1975): 45–83, Plates XXI–XXVIII. doi:10.1179/naw.1975.13.1.005

Chávez, S. J. &. Thompson, R. G. (2006). Early maize on the Copacabana Peninsula: Implications for the archaeology of the Lake Titicaca Basin. In: Staller, J. E., Tykot, R. H., & Benz, B. F. (Eds.) *Histories of Maize: Multidisciplinary Approaches to the Prehistory, Linguistics, Biogeography, Domestication, and Evolution of Maize*, pp. 415–428. Academic Press: New York, NY.

Cieza de León, P. (1984). *La crónica del Perú*. Madrid: Historia, 16(1553), 1880.

Coelho, P. R. P., & McClure, J. E. (2016). The evolution of human cooperation. *Journal of Bioeconomy* 18:65–78.

Cohen, A. B. (2010). Ritual and architecture in the Titicaca Basin: the development of the sunken court complex in the Formative Period. (Order No. 3431799) [Doctoral Dissertation, University of California, Los Angeles] ProQuest Dissertations & Theses Global. www.proquest.com/dissertations-theses/ritual-architecture-titicaca-basin-development/docview/814726623/se-2?accountid=14605

Covey, R. A. (2000). Inka administration of the far south coast of Peru. *Latin American Antiquity* 11: 119–138. doi:10.2307/971851

Covey, R. A. (2006). *How the Incas Built Their Heartland: State Formation and the Innovation of Imperial Strategies in the Sacred Valley, Peru*. University of Michigan Press: Ann Arbor, MI.

Crandall, J. J., & Martin, D. L. (2014). The bioarchaeology of postmortem agency: integrating archaeological theory with human skeletal remains. *Cambridge Archaeological Journal* 24(3): 429–435. doi:10.1017/S0959774314000584

Crumley, C. L. (1979). Three Locational Models: An Epistemological Assessment for Anthropology and Archaeology. In: Schiffer, M. B. (Ed.) *Advances in Archaeological Method and Theory*, pp. 141–173. Academic Press: New York, NY.

Crumley, C. L. (1987). A Dialectical Critique of Hierarchy. In Patterson, T. C. & Gailey, C. W. (Eds.) *Power Relations and State Formation*, pp. 155–169. American Anthropological Association: Washington, DC.

Crumley, C. L. (1995). Heterarchy and the Analysis of Complex Societies. *Archaeological Papers of the American Anthropological Association* 6(1): 1–5. doi:10.1525/ap3a.1995.6.1.1

Crumley, C. L. (2007). Heterarchy. In Darity, W. A. (Ed.) *International Encyclopedia of the Social Sciences*, second edition, pp. 468–469. Macmillian: Detroit.

Darwin, C. (1999 [1839]). *The Voyage of The Beagle*. Wordsworth Classics: Hertfordshire.

Davis, A. R. (2011). *Yuthu: Community and Ritual in an Early Andean Village*. University of Michigan Museum Press: Ann Arbor, MI.

de la Cova, C. (2012). Patterns of trauma and violence in 19th-century-born African American and Euro-American females. *International Journal of Paleopathology* 2(2–3): 61–68. doi:10.1016/j.ijpp.2012.09.009

de la Vega, El Inca Garcilaso. (1966 [1609]). *Historia de la conquista del Nuevo Mundo*. Vol. 3. Madrid: Imprenta de los Hijos de Doña Catalina Piñuela.

Deloria, E. C. (1944). *Speaking of Indians*. Friendship Press: New York, NY.

DeMarrais, E. (2016). Making pacts and cooperative acts: The archaeology of coalition and consensus. *World Archaeology* 48(1): 1–13. doi:10.1080/00438243.2016.1140591

DeMarrais, E., Castillo, L. J., & Earle, T. (1996). Ideology, materialization, and power strategies. *Current Anthropology* 37(1): 15–31. doi:10.1086/204472

Dembo, A., & Imbelloni, J. (1938). *Deformaciones del Cuerpo Humano de Carácter Étnico*. Biblioteca del Americanista Moderno: Buenos Aires.

DeMello, M. (2000). *Bodies of Inscription: A Cultural History of the Modern Tattoo Community*. Duke University Press: Durham, NC.

DeWitte, S. N. (2014). Differential survival among individuals with active and healed periosteal new bone formation. *International Journal of Paleopathology* 7: 38–44. doi:10.1016/j.ijpp.2014.06.001

DeWitte, S. N., & Stojanowski, C. M. (2015). The osteological paradox 20 years later: past perspectives, future directions. *Journal of Archaeological Research* 23(4): 397–450. doi:10.1007/s10814-015-9084-1

Diez de San Miguel, G. (1964 [1567]). *Visita Hecha a la Provincia de Chucuito*. Casa de la Cultura: Lima.

Dransart, P. (2002). *Earth, Water, Fleece and Fabric: an Ethnography and Archaeology of Andean Camelid Herding*. Routledge: London and New York.

Drennan, R. D., & Dai, X. (2010). Chiefdoms and states in the Yuncheng Basin and the Chifeng region: A comparative analysis of settlement systems in North China. *Journal of Anthropological Archaeology* 29(4): 455–468. doi:10.1016/j.jaa.2010.09.001

Duncan, W. N. (2012). Biological Distance Analysis in Contexts of Ritual Violence. In: Martin D. L., Harrod R. P., & Pérez V. R. (Eds.) *The Bioarchaeology of Violence*, pp. 251–275. University Press of Florida: Gainesville.

Earle, T. (1997). *How Chiefs Come to Power*. Stanford University Press: Stanford, CA.

Ehrlich, E., & Maxeiner, H. (2002). External injury marks (wounds) on the head in different types of blunt trauma in an autopsy series. *Medicine and Law* 21:773–782. https://heinonline.org/HOL/P?h=hein.journals/mlv21&i=799

Engelstad, E. (1991). Images of power and contradiction: Feminist theory and post-processual archaeology. *Antiquity* 65(248): 502–14. doi:10.1017/S0003598X00080108

Erickson, C. L. (1993). The social organization of prehispanic raised field agriculture in the Lake Titicaca Basin. In Scarborough, V. & Isaac, B. (Eds.) *Economic Aspects of Water Management in the Prehispanic New World*, pp. 369–426. JAI Press: Greenwich, CT.

Erickson, C. L. (1996). Investigación arqueológica del sistema agrícola de los camellones en la cuenca del lago Titicaca del Perú. Programa Interinstitucional de Waru Waru and Centro para Información para el Desarrollo, La Paz

Erickson, C. L. (2006). Intensification, political economy, and the farming community: In defense of a bottom-up perspective of the past. In: Marcus, J. & Stanish, C. (Eds.) *Agricultural Strategies*, pp. 334–363. Cotsen Institute of Archaeology Press at UCLA: Los Angeles, CA. doi:10.2307/j.ctvdjrr1w.18

Erickson, C., & Candler, K. (1989). Raised fields and sustainable agriculture in the Lake Titicaca Basin. In Browder, J. (Ed.) *Fragile Lands of Latin America: Strategies for Sustainable Development*, pp. 230–248. Westview Press: Boulder, CO.

Ericson, J. E. (1985). Strontium isotope characterization in the study of prehistoric human ecology. *Journal of Human Evolution* 14: 503–514. doi:10.1016/S0047-2484(85)80029-4

Eshed, V, Gopher, A., Pinhasi, R., & Hershkovitz, I. (2010). Paleopathology and the Origin of Agriculture in the Levant. *American Journal of Physical Anthropology* 143:121–133. doi:10.1002/ajpa.21301

Evans-Pritchard, E. E. (1951). *Kinship and Marriage Among the Nuer*. Oxford University Press: Oxford.

Farmer, P. (1999). *Infections and Inequalities: The Modern Plagues*. University of California Press: Berkeley, CA.

Farmer, P. (2003). *Pathologies of Power: Health, Human Rights, and the New War on the Poor*. University of California Press: Berkeley, CA

Feeley-Harnik, G. (1995). Religion and food: an anthropological perspective. *Journal of American Academic Religion* 63(3):565–82.

Fei, H. (1939). *Peasant Life in China: A Field Study of Country Life in the Yangtze Valley*. E.P. Dutton: New York, NY.

Felson, D. T., Lawrence, R. C., Dieppe, P. A., Hirsch, R., Helmick, C. G., Jordan, J. M., Kington, R. S., Lane, N. E., Nevitt, M. C., Zhang, Y., Sowers, M., McAlindon, T., Spector, T. D., Poole, A. R., Yanovski, S. Z., Ateshian, G., Sharma, L., Buckwalter, J. A., Brandt, K. D., & Fries, J. F. (2000). Osteoarthritis: new insights. Part 1: the disease and its risk factors. *Annals of Internal Medicine*, 133(8): 635–646.

Finucane, B., Agurto, P. M., & Isbell, W. H. (2006). Human and animal diet at Conchopata, Peru: stable isotope evidence for maize agriculture and animal management practices during the Middle Horizon. *Journal of Archaeological Science* 33(12): 1766–1776. doi:10.1016/j.jas.2006.03.012

Flannery, K. and J. Marcus (2012). *The Creation of Inequality: How Our Prehistoric Ancestors Set the Stage for Monarchy, Slavery, and Empire*. Harvard University Press: Cambridge, MA.

Franklin, M. (2001). A black feminist-inspired archaeology? *Journal of Social Archaeology* 1(1): 108–125. doi:10.1177/146960530100100108

Fried, M. H. (1967). *The Evolution of Political Society: An Essay in Political Anthropology*. New York: Random House.

Friede, J. (1965). *Descubrimiento y conquista del nuevo reino de Granada: introducción* (No. 2). Ediciones Lerner.

Froehle, A. W., Kellner, C. M., & Schoeninger, M. J. (2012). Multivariate carbon and nitrogen stable isotope model for the reconstruction of prehistoric human diet. *American Journal of Physical Anthropology* 147(3): 352–369. doi:10.1002/ajpa.21651

Geller, P. L. (2004). *Transforming bodies, transforming identities: A consideration of pre-Columbian Maya corporeal beliefs and practices*. Unpublished doctoral dissertation, University of Pennsylvania.

Geller, P. L. (2009). Bodyscapes, biology, and heteronormativity. *American Anthropologist* 111(4): 504–516. doi:10.1111/j.1548-1433.2009.01159.x

Geller, P. L. (2017). *Bioarchaeology of Socio-Sexual Lives*. Springer: Cham, Switzerland.

Glahn, R., Tako, E., & Gore, M. A. (2019). The Germ Fraction Inhibits Iron Bioavailability of Maize: Identification of an Approach to Enhance Maize

Nutritional Quality via Processing and Breeding. *Nutrients* 11(4): 833. doi:10.3390/nu11040833

Goldman, E. (1910) Anarchism: what it really stands for. In: Goldman, E. (Ed.), *Anarchism and Other Essays*, pp. 53–67. Mother Earth Publishing Association: New York, NY.

Goldstein, D. J., Goldstein, R. C. C., & Williams, P. R. (2009). You Are What You Drink. In Jennings, J. & Bowser, B. J. (Eds.), *Drink, Power, and Society in the Andes*, pp.133–166. Gainesville: University Press of Florida.

Goldstein, P. S. (2000). Communities Without Borders: the Vertical Archipelago and Diaspora Communities in the Southern Andes. In Canuto, M. A. & Yaeger, J. (Eds). *The Archaeology of Communities: A New World Perspective*, pp. 182–209. Routledge: New York, NY.

Goldstein, P. S. (2003). From Stew-Eaters to Maize-Drinkers: the Chicha Economy and the Tiwanaku Expansion. In Bray, T. L. (Ed.), *The Archaeology and Politics of Food and Feasting in Early States and Empires*, pp. 143–172. Kluger Academic/Plenum Publishers: New York, NY.

Gómez Mejía, J. (2012). Salud y cambio social: la bioarqueología y su potencial para interpretar el impacto biológico de la agricultura. *Boletín de Antropología Universidad de Antioquia* 26(43): 192–214.

Goodman, A. H. (1998). The Biological Consequences of Inequality in Antiquity. In: Goodman, A. H. & Leatherman, T. L. (Eds.) *Building a New Biocultural Synthesis*, pp 147–170. University of Michigan Press: Ann Arbor, MI.

Goodman, A. H. & Leatherman, T. L. (Eds.) (1998). *Building a New Biocultural Synthesis*. University of Michigan Press: Ann Arbor, MI

Goodman, A. H. & Martin, D. L. (2002). Reconstructing Health Profiles from Skeletal Remains. In: Steckel, R. H. & Rose, J. C. (Eds). *The Backbone of History: Health and Nutrition in the Western Hemisphere*, pp. 11–60. Cambridge University Press: New York, NY.

Goodman, A. H., & Rose, J. C. (1990). Assessment of systemic physiological perturbations from dental enamel hypoplasias and associated histological structures. *American Journal of Physical Anthropology* 33(S11)L 59–110. doi:10.1002/ajpa.1330330506

Graeber D. & Wengrow, D. (2021). *The Dawn of Everything: A New History of Humanity*. Farrar, Straus, and Giroux: New York.

Gregoricka, L. A. (2013). Residential mobility and social identity in the periphery: strontium isotope analysis of archaeological tooth enamel from southeastern Arabia. *Journal of Archaeological Science* 40(1): 452–464. doi:10.1016/j.jas.2012.07.017

Gregoricka, L. A., Ullinger, J., & Sheridan, S. G. (2020). Status, kinship, and place of burial at Early Bronze Age Bab adh-Dhra': A biogeochemical comparison of charnel house human remains. *American Journal of Physical Anthropology* 171(2): 319–335. doi:10.1002/ajpa.23982

Grove, M. J., Baker, P. A., Cross, S. L., Rigsby, C. A., & Seltzer, G. O. (2003). Application of strontium isotopes to understanding the hydrology and paleohydrology of the Altiplano, Bolivia–Peru. *Palaeogeography,*

Palaeoclimatology, Palaeoecology 194(1–3): 281–297. doi:10.1016/S0031-0182(03)00282-7

Haas, R., & Viviano Llave, C. (2015). Hunter-gatherers on the eve of agriculture: investigations at Soro Mik'aya Patjxa, Lake Titicaca Basin, Peru, 8000-6700 BP. *Antiquity* 89(348), 1297–1312. doi:10.15184/aqy.2015.100

Halcrow, S. E. & Tayles, N. (2011). The Bioarchaeological Investigation of Children and Childhood. In: Agarwal, S. C. & Glencross, B.A. (Eds.) *Social Bioarchaeology*, pp. 333–360. Wiley-Blackwell: Oxford.

Harrod, R. P., & Martin, D. L. (2014). Climate Change, Social Control and Violence in the US Southwest. In: Harrod, R. P. & Martin, D. L. (Eds.) *Bioarchaeology of Climate Change and Violence*, pp. 33–58. SpringerBriefs in Anthropology. Springer, New York, NY. https://doi.org/10.1007/978-1-4614-9239-9_4

Hastorf, C. A. 2003. Community with the ancestors: ceremonies and social memory in the Middle Formative at Chiripa, Bolivia. *Journal of Anthropological Archaeology* 22: 305–332. doi:10.1016/S0278-4165(03)00029-1

Hastorf, C. A. 2005. The Upper (Middle and Late) Formative in the Titicaca Region. In: Stanish, C., Cohen, A. B. & Aldenderfer, M. S. (Eds.) *Advances in Titicaca Basin Archaeology-1* pp. 65–94. Cotsen Institute of Archaeology at UCLA: Los Angeles, CA.

Hatch, M. A. (2012). Meaning and the Bioarchaeology of Captivity, Sacrifice, and Cannibalism: A Case Study from the Mississippian Period at Larson, Illinois. In Martin D.L., Harrod R.P., & Pérez V.R. (Eds.) *The Bioarchaeolgoy of Violence*, pp. 201–225. University Press of Florida: Gainesville.

Henry, E. R., Angelbeck, B., & Rizvi, U. Z. (2017). Against typology: A critical approach to archaeological order. *The SAA Archaeological Record* 17(1): 28–32. https://hdl.handle.net/1887/67984

Hillson, S. (2008). *Dental Anthropology*. Cambridge University Press: Cambridge.

Hoshower, L. M., Buikstra, J. E., Goldstein, P. S., & Webster, A. D. (1995). Artificial cranial deformation at the Omo M10 site: A Tiwanaku complex from the Moquegua Valley, Peru. *Latin American Antiquity* 6(2): 145–164. doi:10.2307/972149

Hu, D., & Quave, K. E. (2020). Prosperity and prestige: Archaeological realities of unfree laborers under Inka imperialism. *Journal of Anthropological Archaeology* 59: 101201. doi:10.1016/j.jaa.2020.101201

Isbell, W. H. (2000). What we should be studying: the "imagined community" and the "natural community". In: Canuto, M. A. & Yaeger, J. (Eds). *The Archaeology of Communities: A New World Perspective*, pp. 243–266. Routledge: New York, NY.

Janusek, J. W. I2008). *Ancient Tiwanaku*. Cambridge University Press: New York, NY.

Johnson, K. M., & Paul, K. S. (2016). Bioarchaeology and kinship: integrating theory, social relatedness, and biology in ancient family research. *Journal of Archaeological Research*, 24(1): 75–123. doi:10.1007/s10814-015-9086-z

Joyce, R. A. (2017). Sex, gender, and anthropology. In: Agarwal, S. C. & Wesp, J. K. (Eds.) *Exploring Sex and Gender in Bioarchaeology*, pp. 1–14. University of New Mexico Press: Albuquerque, NM.

Judd, M. A. (2008). The parry problem. *Journal of Archaeological Science*, 35(6): 1658–1666. doi:10.1016/j.jas.2007.11.005

Juengst, S. (2017). Inclusive Communities in The Titicaca Basin During the Early Horizon. *Archaeological Papers of the American Anthropological Association* 28(1): 24–37. doi.org/10.1111/apaa.12086

Juengst, S. L. (2018). Complexity and power: A bioarchaeological analysis of socioeconomic change on the Copacabana peninsula, 800 BC–AD 200. *Bioarchaeology International* 2(1): 1–19. doi:10.5744/bi.2018.1013.

Juengst, S. L. (2020). A diachronic view of violent relations and environmental change in the Titicaca Basin, Bolivia. In: Schug, G.R. (Ed.) *The Routledge Handbook of the Bioarchaeology of Climate and Environmental Change*, pp. 345–363. Routledge: New York, NY.

Juengst, S. L., & Chávez, S. J. (2015). Three trepanned skulls from the Copacabana Peninsula in the Titicaca Basin, Bolivia (800 BC–AD 1000). *International Journal of Paleopathology*, 9: 20–27.

Juengst, S. L., Chávez, S. J., Hutchinson, D. L., & Chávez, S. R. (2017a). Late Preceramic forager–herders from the Copacabana Peninsula in the Titicaca Basin of Bolivia: A bioarchaeological analysis. *International Journal of Osteoarchaeology* 27(3): 430–440. doi:10.1002/oa.2566

Juengst, S. L., Hutchinson, D. L., Chávez, K. M., Chávez, S. J., Chávez, S. R., Krigbaum, J., Schober, T. & Norr, L., (2021). The resiliency of diet on the Copacabana Peninsula, Bolivia. *Journal of Anthropological Archaeology* 61:101260. doi:10.1016/j.jaa.2020.101260.

Junghanns, H., & Schmorl, G. (1971). *The Human Spine in Health and Disease*. Grune & Stratton: New York, NY.

Jurmain, R. (2013). *Stories from the Skeleton: Behavioral Reconstruction in Human Osteology*, 2nd edition. Routledge: New York, NY.

Jurmain, R., Cardoso, F.A., Henderson, C. & Villotte, S. (2011). Bioarchaeology's Holy Grail: The Reconstruction of Activity. In: Grauer, A. L. (Ed.) *A Companion to Paleopathology*, pp. 531–552. John Wiley & Sons: Malden, MA. doi:10.1002/9781444345940.ch29

Kellner, C. M., & Schoeninger, M. J. (2007). A simple carbon isotope model for reconstructing prehistoric human diet. *American Journal of Physical Anthropology* 133(4): 1112–1127. doi:10.1002/ajpa.20618

Kent, Jonathan D. (1982). The domestication and exploitation of the South American camelids: methods of analysis and their application to circumlacustrine archaeological sites in Bolivia and Peru. (Order No. 8223797) [Doctoral Dissertation, Washington University]. ProQuest Dissertations & Theses Global. www.proquest.com/dissertations-theses/domestication-exploitation-south-american/docview/303082674/se-2?accountid=14605

Kent, S. (1986). The influence of sedentism and aggregation on porotic hyperostosis and anaemia: A case study. *Man* 21(4), 605–636. doi:10.2307/2802900

Keswani, P. S. (1989). Dimensions of social hierarchy in Late Bronze Age Cyprus: an analysis of the mortuary data from Enkomi. *Journal of Mediterranean Archaeology* 2(1):49–86.

Kitchel, N., Aldenderfer, M.S. & Haas, R. (2021). Diet, mobility, technology, and lithics: Neolithization on the Andean Altiplano, 7.0–3.5 ka. *Journal of Archaeological Method & Theory*. doi:10.1007/s10816-021-09525-7

Klaus, H. D. (2012). The bioarchaeology of structural violence: A theoretical model and a case study. In Martin, D.L., Harrod, R.P., Perez, V.R. (Eds.) *The Bioarchaeology of Violence*, pp. 29–62. University Press of Florida; Gainesville.

Klaus, H. D., & Tam, M. E. (2009). Contact in the Andes: Bioarchaeology of systemic stress in colonial Mórrope, Peru. *American Journal of Physical Anthropology* 138(3): 356–368. doi:10.1002/ajpa.20944

Klaus, H. D., Harvey, A. R., & Cohen, M. N. (2017). *Bones of Complexity: Bioarchaeological Case Studies of Social Organization and Skeletal Biology*. University Press of Florida: Gainesville, FL.

Klesse, C. (1999). Modern primitivism': non-mainstream body modification and racialized representation. *Body & Society* 5(2–3): 15–38. doi:10.1177/1357034X99005002002

Knudson, K. J. (2004). Tiwanaku residential mobility in the south central Andes: Identifying archaeological human migration through strontium isotope analysis. (Order No. 3127987). [Doctoral Dissertation, University of Wisconsin, Madison]. ProQuest Dissertations & Theses Global. (305109799). www.proquest.com/dissertations-theses/tiwanaku-residential-mobility-south-central-andes/docview/305109799/se-2?accoun tid=14605

Knudson, K. J. (2008). Tiwanaku influence around the south central Andes: Strontium isotope analysis and middle horizon migration. *Latin American Antiquity* 19(1): 3–23. doi:10.1017/S104566350000763X

Knudson, K. J. & Tung, T. A. (2011). Investigating regional mobility in the southern hinterland of the Wari Empire: Biogeochemistry at the site of Beringa, Peru. *American Journal of Physical Anthropology* 145: 299–310. doi:10.1002/ajpa.21494

Kolata, A. L. (1993). *The Tiwanaku: Portrait of an Andean Civilization*. Blackwell: Cambridge.

Kolb, M. J. (1997). Labor mobilization, ethnohistory, and the archaeology of community in Hawai'i. *Journal of Archaeological Method and Theory* 4: 265–285. doi:10.1007/BF02428064

Kolb, M. J. & Snead, J. (1997). It's a small world after all: Comparative analysis of community organization in archaeology. *American Antiquity* 64(4): 609–628. doi:10.2307/281881

Konigsberg, L. W. (1990). Analysis of prehistoric biological variation under a model of isolation by geographic and temporal distance. *Human Biology* 62: 49–70.

Kremer, C., Racette, S., Dionne, C.-A. and Sauvageau, A. (2008), Discrimination of Falls and Blows in Blunt Head Trauma: Systematic Study of the Hat Brim Line Rule in Relation to Skull Fractures. *Journal of Forensic Sciences* 53: 716–719. doi:10.1111/j.1556-4029.2008.00725.x

Kristiansen, K. (2010). Decentralized Complexity: The Case of Bronze Age Northern Europe. In Price T. D., Feinman G. M. (Eds.) *Pathways to Power. Fundamental Issues in Archaeology*, pp. 169–192. Springer: New York, NY. doi:10.1007/978-1-4419-6300-0_7

Krohn-Hansen, C. (1994). The anthropology of violent interaction. *Journal of Anthropological Research* 50(4): 367–381. doi.10.1086/jar.50.4.3630559

Kuckelman, K. A., & Martin, D. L. (2012). Taphonomy and warfare in the Mesa Verde region. *Landscapes of Violence* 2(2): 13. doi: 10.7275/R5D798BW

Kuzminsky, S. C., Tung, T. A., Hubbe, M., & Villaseñor-Marchal, A. (2016). The application of 3D geometric morphometrics and laser surface scanning to investigate the standardization of cranial vault modification in the Andes. *Journal of Archaeological Science: Reports* 10: 507–513. doi:10.1016/j.jasrep.2016.11.007

Kyle, B., & Reitsema, L. (2020). Social variation in an urban environment and its impacts on stress: Preliminary results from Ancient Greek Himera (Sicily). In: Schug, G. R. (Ed.) *The Routledge Handbook of the Bioarchaeology of Climate and Environmental Change*, pp. 205–220. Routledge: New York, NY.

Larsen, C. S. (1995). Biological changes in human populations with agriculture. *Annual Review of Anthropology* 24: 185–213. doi:10.1146/annurev.an.24.100195.001153

Larsen, C. S. (2015). *Bioarchaeology: Interpreting Behavior from the Human Skeleton*. Cambridge University Press: Cambridge.

Lee-Thorp, J. A., Sealy, J. C., & Van Der Merwe, N. J. (1989). Stable carbon isotope ratio differences between bone collagen and bone apatite, and their relationship to diet. *Journal of Archaeological Science* 16(6): 585–599. doi:10.1016/0305-4403(89)90024-1

Levine, A. R. (2012). *Competition, Cooperation, and the Emergence of Regional Centers in the Northern Lake Titicaca Basin, Peru*. eScholarship, University of California.

Lévi-Strauss, C. (1983). *The Way of the Masks*. Translated by Modelski, S. Jonathan Cape: London.

Levy, J. E. (1995). Heterarchy in Bronze Age Denmark: Settlement pattern, gender, and ritual. *Archeological Papers of the American Anthropological Association* 6(1): 41–53. doi:10.1525/ap3a.1995.6.1.41

Levy, J. E. (2012). Gender, power, and heterarchy in middle-level societies. In: Sweely, T. L. (Ed.) *Manifesting Power*, pp. 76–92. Routledge: New York, NY.

References

Lewis, M. E. (2007). *The bioarchaeology of children: perspectives from biological and forensic anthropology*. Cambridge University Press.

Logan, A. L., Hastorf, C. A., & Pearsall, D. M. (2012). "Let's Drink Together": Early ceremonial use of maize in the Titicaca Basin. *Latin American Antiquity* 23(3): 235–258. doi:10.7183/1045-6635.23.3.235

Lovell, N. C. (1997). Trauma analysis in paleopathology. *American Journal of Physical Anthropology* 104(S25): 139–170. doi:10.1002/(SICI)1096-8644(1997)25+<139::AID-AJPA6>3.0.CO;2-%23

Lowman, S. A., Sharratt, N., & Turner, B. L. (2019). Bioarchaeology of social transition: A diachronic study of pathological conditions at Tumilaca la Chimba, Peru. *International Journal of Osteoarchaeology* 29(1): 62–72. doi:10.1002/oa.2713

Lozada, M. C., & Buikstra, J. E. (2002). *El Señorío de Chiribaya en la costa sur del Perú*. Instituto de Estudios Peruanos: Lima.

Maestripieri, D. (1999). The biology of human parenting: insights from non-human primates. *Neuroscience & Biobehavioral Reviews* 23(3): 411–422. doi:10.1016/S0149-7634(98)00042-6

Malinowski, B. (1913). *The Family among the Australian Aborigines: A Sociological Study* (Vol. 2). London: University of London Press.

Mannheim, B., Davis, A. R., & Velasco, M. C. (2018). Cranial Modification in the Central Andes. In Tiesler, V. & Lozada, M. C. (Eds). *Social Skins of the Head: Body Beliefs and Ritual in Ancient Mesoamerica and the Andes*, pp. 223–234. Albuquerque: University of New Mexico Press.

Marc-Antoine, V., & Nicolas, L. (2021). Geomorphological map of the Tiwanaku River watershed in Bolivia: Implications for past and present human occupation. *CATENA* 206: 105508. doi:10.1016/j.catena.2021.105508

Marcus, J. (2000). Toward an archaeology of communities. In: Canuto, M. A. & Yaeger, J. (Eds). *The Archaeology of Communities: A New World Perspective*, pp. 231–42. Routledge: New York, NY.

Marquez Morfin, L. (1998). Unequal in death as in life: a sociopolitical analysis of the 1813 Mexico City typhus epidemic. In: Goodman, A. H. & Leatherman, T. L. (Eds.) *Building a New Biocultural Synthesis*, pp. 229–244. University of Michigan Press: Ann Arbor, MI.

Martin, D. L., & Frayer, T. (1997). *Troubled Times: Osteological and Anthropological Evidence of Violence*. Gordon and Breach Publishing: Amsterdam.

Martin, D. L., & Harrod, R. P. (2015). Bioarchaeological contributions to the study of violence. *American Journal of Physical Anthropology* 156: 116–145. doi:10.1002/ajpa.22662

Martin, D. L., Harrod, R. P., & Pérez, V. R. (2012). *The Bioarchaeology of Violence*. University Press of Florida: Gainesville, FL.

McDade, T. W., Reyes-García, V., Tanner, S., Huanca, T., & Leonard, W. R. (2008). Maintenance versus growth: Investigating the costs of immune activation among children in lowland Bolivia. *American Journal of Physical Anthropology* 136(4): 478–484. doi:10.1002/ajpa.20831

McIlvaine, B. K. (2015). Implications of Reappraising the Iron-Deficiency Anemia Hypothesis. *International Journal of Osteoarchaeology* 25(6): 997–1000. doi:10.1002/oa.2383

McKinnon, S. (1991). *From a Shattered Sun: Hierarchy, Gender, and Alliance in the Tanimbar Islands*. University of Wisconsin Press: Madison, WI.

Mead, M. (1934). *Kinship in the Admiralty Islands*. Routledge: New York, NY

Mead, M. (1937). *Cooperation and Competition among Primitive Peoples*. McGraw Hill: New York, NY.

Meindl, R. S. & Lovejoy, C. O. (1985). Ectocranial suture closure: A revised method for the determination of skeletal age at death based on the lateral-anterior sutures. *American Journal of Physical Anthropology* 69:57–66. doi:10.1002/ajpa.1330680106.

Meyer, C., Ganslmeier, R., Dresely, V., & Alt, K. W. (2012). New approaches to the reconstruction of kinship and social structure based on bioarchaeological analysis of Neolithic multiple and collective graves. In: Kolář, J., & Trampota, F. (Eds.) *Theoretical and Methodological Considerations in Central European Neolithic Archaeology*, pp. 11–23. Oxford BAR International Series 2325.

Miller, M. J., Capriles, J. M., & Hastorf, C. A. (2010). The fish of Lake Titicaca: implications for archaeology and changing ecology through stable isotope analysis. *Journal of Archaeological Science* 37(2): 317–327. doi:10.1016/j.jas.2009.09.043

Miller, M. J., Kendall, I., Capriles, J. M., Bruno, M. C., Evershed, R. P., & Hastorf, C. A. (2021). Quinoa, potatoes, and llamas fueled emergent social complexity in the Lake Titicaca Basin of the Andes. *Proceedings of the National Academy of Sciences* 118(49): e2113395118.doi:10.1073/pnas.2113395118

Mintz, S. & Du Bois, C. M. (2002). The Anthropology of Food and Eating. *Annual Review of Anthropology* 31: 99–119. doi:10.1146/annurev.anthro.32.032702.131011

Montgomery, R.T. & Perry, M. (2012). The social and cultural implications of violence at Qasr Hallabut. In: Martin, D.E., Harrod, R.P. & Pérez, V. R. (eds.) *The Bioarchaeology of Violence*, pp. 83–110. University Press of Florida: Gainesville, FL.

Moore, K. M. (2011). Grace under pressure: responses to changing environments by herders and fishers in the Formative Lake Titicaca Basin, Bolivia. In: Miller, N. F., Moore, K. M. & Ryan K. (Eds.), *Sustainable Lifeways*, pp. 244–272. University of Pennsylvania Press: Philadelphia, PA.

Moore, K. M. (2016). Early domesticated camelids in the Andes. In: Capriles, J.M. & Tripcevich N. (eds). *The Archaeology of Andean Pastoralism*, pp. 17–38. University of New Mexico Press: Albuquerque, NM.

Moore, K. M., Steadman, D., deFrance, S., (1999). Herds, fish, and fowl in the domestic and ritual economy of Formative Chiripa. In: Hastorf, C. A. (Ed.), *Early Settlement at Chiripa, Bolivia. Research of the Taraco Archaeological Project*, pp. 105–166. Contributions of the Archaeological Research Facility 57, Berkeley, CA.

Moore, K. M., Bruno, M. C., Capriles, J. M., & Hastorf, C. A. (2007). Integrated contextual approaches to understanding past activities using plant and animal remains from Kala Uyuni. In: Bandy, M. & Hastorf, C.A. (Eds.) *Kala Uyuni: an early political center in the southern Lake Titicaca basin,* pp. 173–203. Contributions of the Archaeological Research Facility 57: Berkeley, CA.

Morgan, L. H. (2013 [1877]). *Ancient Society.* Harvard University Press: Cambridge, MA.

Murphy, T. R. (1959). The Changing Pattern of Dentine Exposure in Human Tooth Attrition. *American Journal of Physical Anthropology* 17: 167–178. doi:10.1002/ajpa.1330170302

Murra, J. V. (1980). *The Economic Organization of the Inca State.* Research in Economic Anthropology, Supplement 1. JAI Press: Greenwich.

Murra, J. V. (1985). El Archipelago Vertical Revisted, and Limits and Limitations of the 'Vertical Archipelago' in the Andes. In: Masuda, S., Shimada, I. & Morris, C. (Eds.) *Andean Ecology and Civilization,* pp. 15–20. University of Tokyo Press: Tokyo.

Murray, A. P. (2005). *Chenopodium* domestication in the South-Central Andes: Confirming the presence of domesticates at Jiskairumoko (Late Archaic-Formative), Peru. MA Thesis, Department of Anthropology, California State University, Fullerton.

Navas, C. (1997). Thermal extremes at high elevations in the Andes: Physiological ecology of frogs. *Journal of Thermal Biology* 22: 467–477. doi:10.1016/S0306-4565(97)00065-X

O'Brien, T. G., & Stanley, A. M. (2013). Boards and cords: discriminating types of artificial cranial deformation in prehispanic South Central Andean populations. *International Journal of Osteoarchaeology* 23(4): 459–470. doi:10.1002/oa.1269

O'Connell, T. C., Kneale, C. J., Tasevska, N., & Kuhnle, G. G. (2012). The diet-body offset in human nitrogen isotopic values: A controlled dietary study. *American Journal of Physical Anthropology* 149(3): 426–434. doi.org/10.1002/ajpa.22140

Okumura, M. (2014). Differences in types of artificial cranial deformation are related to differences in frequencies of cranial and oral health markers in pre-Columbian skulls from Peru. Boletim do Museu Paraense Emílio Goeldi. *Ciências Humanas* 9: 15–26. doi:10.1590/S1981-81222014000100002

Orlove, Ben. (2002). *Lines in the Water: Nature and Culture at Lake Titicaca.* University of California Press: Berkeley, CA.

Ortner, D. J. (2003). *Identification of Pathological Conditions in Human Skeletal Remains.* Academic Press: New York, NY.

Ortner, D. J. (2011). Human skeletal paleopathology. *International Journal of Paleopathology* 1(1): 4–11. doi:10.1016/j.ijpp.2011.01.002

Ottenheimer, M. (1995). Why is there no Kinship, Daddy?. *Human Mosaic,* 28(2), 65–72.

Oxenham, M. F., & Cavill, I. (2010). Porotic Hyperostosis and Cribra Orbitalia: The Erythropoietic Response to Iron-Deficiency Anaemia. *Anthropological Science* 118(3): 199–200. doi:10.1537/ase.100302

Parker Pearson, M. (2003). *The Archaeology of Death and Burial*, 2nd ed. Sutton Publishing Ltd: Stroud.

Patrucco, R., Tello, R., & Bonavia, D. (1983). Parasitological Studies of Coprolites of Pre-Hispanic Peruvian Populations. *Current Anthropology* 24(3): 393–394. doi:10.1086/203016

Paynter, R. (1989). The archaeology of equality and inequality. *Annual Review of Anthropology*, 18: 369–399.

Pearson, O. M., Buikstra, J. E. (2006). Behavior and the bones. In: Buikstra, J. E., Beck, L. A. (Eds.), *Bioarchaeology: The Contextual Analysis of Human Remains*, pp. 207–225. Elsevier: Amsterdam.

Pechenkina, E. A., & Delgado, M. (2006). Dimensions of health and social structure in the early intermediate period cemetery at Villa El Salvador, Peru. *American Journal of Physical Anthropology* 131(2): 218–235. doi:10.1002/ajpa.20432

Pérez, V. R. (2012). The Politicization of the Dead: Violence as Performance, Politics, as Usual. In: Martin, D. E., Harrod, R. P. & Pérez, V. R. (Eds.) *The Bioarchaeology of Violence*, pp. 13–28. University Press of Florida: Gainesville, FL.

Phenice, T. W. 1969. A newly developed visual model of sexing the os pubis. *American Journal of Physical Anthropology* 30:297–301. doi:10.1002/ajpa.1330300214.

Pilloud, M. A., & Larsen, C. S. (2011). "Official" and "practical" kin: Inferring social and community structure from dental phenotype at Neolithic Çatalhöyük, Turkey. *American Journal of Physical Anthropology* 145(4): 519–530. doi:10.1002/ajpa.21520

Pomeroy, E., Stock, J. T., Zakrzewski, S. R., & Lahr, M. M. (2010). A metric study of three types of artificial cranial modification from north-central Peru. *International Journal of Osteoarchaeology* 20(3): 317–334. doi:10.1002/oa.1044

Ponce, P. V. (2010). *A comparative study of activity-related skeletal changes in 3rd-2nd millennium BC coastal fishers and 1st millenium AD inland agriculturists in Chile, South America*. Unpublished doctoral dissertation, Department of Archaeology, Durham University.

Price, T. D., & Bar-Yosef, O. (2010). Traces of inequality at the origins of agriculture in the ancient Near East. In Pathways to Power (pp. 147–168). Springer, New York, NY.

Price, T. D., J. H. Burton, and R. Alexander Bentley (2002). The Characterization of Biologically Available Strontium Isotope Ratios for the Study of Prehistoric Migration. *Archaeometry* 44:117–136.

Rautman, A. E. (2016). 'Circling the wagons' and community formation: interpreting circular villages in the archaeological record. *World Archaeology* 48(1): 125–143. https://doi.org/10.1080/00438243.2015.1101395

Redfern, R. & Chamberlain, A. (2011). A demographic analysis of Maiden Castle hillfort: evidence for conflict in the late Iron Age and early Roman period. *International Journal of Paleopathology* 1: 68–73. doi:10.1016/j.ijpp.2011.02.004

Redfern, R. (2020). Making sense of violence and environmental change in Europe. In: Schug, G. R. (Ed.) *The Routledge Handbook of the Bioarchaeology of Climate and Environmental Change*, pp. 279–300. Routledge: London.

Rhode, M. P. (2006). *Habitual subsistence practices among prehistoric Andean populations: fishers and farmers*. Unpublished doctoral dissertation, Department of Anthropology, University of Missouri-Columbia. doi:10.32469/10355/4374

Riches, D. (Ed.). (1986). *The Anthropology of Violence*. Basil Blackwell: New York, NY.

Roberts, C. A., & Manchester, K. (2007). *The Archaeology of Disease*, 3rd Edition. Cornell University Press: Ithaca, NY.

Roddick, A. P. & Hastorf, C. A. (2010). Tradition brought to the surface: continuity, innovation, and change in the Late Formative Period, Taraco Peninsula, Bolivia. *Cambridge Archaeological* Journal 20(2):157–178. doi:10.1017/S0959774310000211

Rogers, J., & Waldron, T. (1995). *A Field Guide to Joint Disease in Archaeology*. John Wiley & Sons: Malden, MA.

Rothschild, B. (2002). Porotic hyperostosis as a marker of health and nutritional conditions. *American Journal of Human Biology* 14(4): 417–418. doi:10.1002/ajhb.10078

Sahlins, M. (2013). *What Kinship Is—And Is Not*. University of Chicago Press: Chicago, IL.

Sapolsky, R. (2004). *Why Zebras Don't Get Ulcers*. Henry Holt and Company: New York, NY.

Scaffidi, B. K., & Knudson, K. J. (2020). An archaeological strontium isoscape for the prehistoric Andes: Understanding population mobility through a geostatistical meta-analysis of archaeological 87Sr/86Sr values from humans, animals, and artifacts. *Journal of Archaeological Science*, 117: 105121.

Scheper-Hughes, N. & Bourgois, P. (2004). Introduction: making sense of violence. In: Scheper-Hughes, N. & Bourgois, P. (Eds.) *Violence in War and Peace*, pp. 1–12. Blackwell Publishing: Malden.

Schoeninger, M. J., & DeNiro, M. J. (1984). Nitrogen and carbon isotopic composition of bone collagen from marine and terrestrial animals. *Geochimica et Cosmochimica Acta* 48(4): 625–639. doi:10.1016/0016-7037(84)90091-7

Schoeninger, M. J., & Moore, K. (1992). Bone stable isotope studies in archaeology. *Journal of World Prehistory* 6(2), 247–296. doi:10.1007/BF00975551

Schrader, S. (2019). *Activity, Diet and Social Practice: Addressing Everyday Life in Human Skeletal Remains*. Springer Nature Switzerland: Cham.

Scott, G. R. & Turner II, C. (1988). Dental anthropology. *Annual Review of Anthropology* 17: 99–126. doi:10.1146/annurev.an.17.100188.000531

Scrimshaw, N. S. (2003). Historical concepts of interactions, synergism and antagonism between nutrition and infection. *The Journal of Nutrition* 133(1): 316S–321S. doi:10.1093/jn/133.1.316S

Scrimshaw, N. S., Taylor, C. E., & Gordon, J. E. (1959). Interactions of nutrition and infection. *American Journal of Medical Sciences* 237(3): 367–403.

Service, E. R. (1962). *Primitive Social Organization*. Random House: New York, NY.

Shapiro, W. (2014). Contesting Marshall Sahlins on Kinship. *Oceania* 84(1): 19–37. doi:10.1002/ocea.5033

Sharpe, A. E., Emery, K. F., Inomata, T., Triadan, D., Kamenov, G. D., & Krigbaum, J. (2018). Earliest isotopic evidence in the Maya region for animal management and long-distance trade at the site of Ceibal, Guatemala. *Proceedings of the National Academy of Sciences* 115(14): 3605–3610. doi:10.1073/pnas.1713880115

Shuler, K. A. (2011). Life and death on a Barbadian sugar plantation: historic and bioarchaeological views of infection and mortality at Newton Plantation. *International Journal of Osteoarchaeology* 21(1): 66–81. doi:10.1002/oa.1108

Shults, A. J. (2020). *Activity and mobility during the terminal Archaic period in the eastern Andes: A bioarchaeological analysis* (Order No. 27964759). ProQuest Dissertations & Theses Global. www.proquest.com/dissertations-theses/activity-mobility-during-terminal-archaic-period/docview/2406591670/se-2?accountid=14605

Slovak, N. M. & Paytan, A. (2011). Applications of Sr isotopes in archaeology. In: Baskaran, M. (Ed.) *Handbook of Environmental Isotope Geochemistry*, pp. 743–768. Springer-Verlag: Berlin Heidelberg. doi:10.1007/978-3-642-10637-835

Smith, B. H. (1984). Patterns of molar wear in hunter-gatherers and agriculturalists. *American Journal of Physical Anthropology* 63: 39–56. doi:10.1002/ajpa.1330630107

Smith, B. N., & Epstein, S. (1971). Two categories of $^{13}C/^{12}C$ ratios for higher plants. *Plant Physiology* 47(3): 380–384. doi:10.1104/pp.47.3.380

Smith, H. J. (2009). *Parenting for Primates*. Harvard University Press: Cambridge, MA.

Sofaer, J. R. (2006). *The Body as Material Culture: A Theoretical Osteoarchaeology*. Cambridge University Press: Cambridge.

Sofaer, J. R. (2011). Towards a social bioarchaeology of age. In Agarwal, S. C. & Glencross, B. A. (Eds.) *Social Bioarchaeology*, pp. 285–311. Wiley-Blackwell: Oxford.

Spencer-Wood, S. M. (2010) A feminist framework for analyzing powered cultural landscapes in historical archaeology. *International Journal of Historical Archaeology* 14: 498–526. doi:10.1007/s10761-010-0122-x

Stanish, C. (2003). *Ancient Titicaca*. University of California Press: Los Angeles, CA.

Stanish, C. (2004). The evolution of chiefdoms: An economic anthropological model. In: Feinman, G. & Nicholas, L. (Eds.) *Archaeological Perspectives on Political Economies*, pp. 7–24. University of Utah Press: Salt Lake City, UT.
Stanish, C. (2017). *The Evolution of Human Co-operation*. Cambridge: Cambridge University Press.
Stanish, C., & Levine, A. (2011). War and early state formation in the northern Titicaca Basin, Peru. *Proceedings of the National Academy of Sciences*, 108(34): 13901–13906.
Stanish, C., Burger, R. L., Cipolla, L. M., Glascock, M. D. & Quelima, E. (2002). Evidence for early long-distance obsidian exchange and watercraft use from the Southern Lake Titicaca Basin of Bolivia and Peru. *Latin American Antiquity* 13(4): 444–454. doi:10.2307/972225
Stojanowski, C. & Buikstra, J. E. (2004). Biodistance analysis, a biocultural enterprise: A rejoinder to Armelagos and Van Gerven (2003). *American Anthropologist* 106(2): 430–431. doi:10.1525/aa.2004.106.2.430
Stojanowski, C. M. & Schillaci, M. A. (2006). Phenotypic approaches for understanding patterns of intracemetery biological variation. *Yearbook of Physical Anthropology* 49: 49–88. doi:10.1002/ajpa.20517
Stone, P. K. (2012). Binding women: Ethnology, skeletal deformations, and violence against women. *International Journal of Paleopathology* 2(2-3): 53–60. doi:10.1016/j.ijpp.2012.09.008
Stone, P. K., & Sanders, L. S. (2020). *Bodies and Lives in Victorian England: Science, Sexuality, and the Affliction of Being Female*. Routledge: New York, NY.
Stuart-Macadam, P. (1985). Porotic hyperostosis: Representative of a childhood condition. *American Journal of Physical Anthropology* 66(4): 391–398. doi:10.1002/ajpa.1330660407
Stuart-Macadam, P. (1992). Porotic hyperostosis: A new perspective. *American Journal of Physical Anthropology* 87(1): 39–47. doi:10.1002/ajpa.1330870105
Suby, J. A. (2020). Paleopathological research in Southern Patagonia: An approach to understanding stress and disease in hunter-gatherer populations. *Latin American Antiquity* 31(2): 392–408. doi:10.1017/laq.2020.5
Suchey, J. & Katz, D. (1986). Skeletal Age Standards Derives from Extensive Multiracial Sample of Modern Americans. *American Journal of Physical Anthropology* 69: 269.
Sutter, R. C. (2000). Prehistoric genetic and culture change: A bioarchaeological search for pre-Inka altiplano colonies in the coastal valleys of Moquegua, Peru, and Azapa, Chile. *Latin American Antiquity* 11(1): 43–70. doi:10.2307/1571670
Sutter R. C. & Verano, J. W. (2006). Biodistance analysis of the Moche sacrificial victims from Huaca de la Luna plaza 3C: matrix method test of their origins. *American Journal of Physical Anthropology* 132(2): 39–47. doi:10.1002/ajpa.20514

Sutter, R. C. & Cortez, R. J. (2005). The Nature of Moche Human Sacrifice: A Bio-Archaeological Perspective. *Current Anthropology* 46(4): 521–549. doi:10.1086/431527

Swedlund, A. C. & Ball, H. (1998). Nature, Nurture, and the Determinants of Infant Mortality: A Case Study from Massachusetts, 1830–1920. In: Goodman, A. H. & Leatherman, T. L. (Eds.) *Building a New Biocultural Synthesis*, pp. 191–228. University of Michigan Press: Ann Arbor, MI.

Szpak, P., Millaire, J. F., White, C. D., & Longstaffe, F. J. (2014). Small scale camelid husbandry on the north coast of Peru (Virú Valley): Insight from stable isotope analysis. *Journal of Anthropological Archaeology* 36: 110–129. doi:10.1016/j.jaa.2014.08.005

Te Awekotuku, N. (2003). Ta Moko: Culture, body modification, and the psychology of identity. In: Nikora, L. W., Levy, M., Masters, B., Waitoki, W., Te Awekotuku, N., & Etheredge, R. J. M. (Eds). *Tatau/Tattoo: Embodied Art and Cultural Exchange c. 1760–2000*, pp. 123–127. Maori and Psychology Research Unit, University of Waikato: Hamilton, NZ. https://hdl.handle.net/10289/869

Temple, D. H., & Goodman, A. H. (2014). Bioarcheology has a "health" problem: Conceptualizing "stress" and "health" in bioarcheological research. *American Journal of Physical Anthropology* 155(2): 186–191. doi:10.1002/ajpa.22602

Tiesler, V. (2013). *The Bioarchaeology of Artificial Cranial Modifications: New Approaches to Head Shaping and its Meanings in Pre-Columbian Mesoamerica and Beyond*. Springer Science & Business Media: New York, NY.

Titelbaum, A. R. (2012). Habitual activity and changing adaptations at the El Brujo archaeological complex: a diachronic investigation of musculoskeletal stress and degenerative joint disease in the lower Chicama valley of northern coastal Peru. Unpublished Doctoral dissertation. Department of Anthropology, Tulane University, New Orleans.

Todd, T. W. (1921a). Age changes in the pubic bone I: the male white pubis. *American Journal of Physical Anthropology* 3: 285–334.

Todd, T. W. (1921b) Age changes in the pubis bone III: The pubis of the white female. IV. The pubis of the female White-Negro Hybrid. *American Journal of Physical Anthropology* 4: 1–70.

Torres-Rouff, C. (2002). Cranial vault modification and ethnicity in middle horizon San Pedro de Atacama, Chile. *Current Anthropolog*, 43(1): 163–171. doi:10.1086/338290

Torres-Rouff, C. (2008). The influence of Tiwanaku on life in the Chilean Atacama: mortuary and bodily perspectives. *American Anthropologist* 110(3): 325–337. doi:10.1111/j.1548-1433.2008.00042.x

Torres-Rouff, C. (2020). Cranial modification and the shapes of heads across the Andes. *International Journal of Paleopathology* 29: 94–101. doi:10.1016/j.ijpp.2019.06.007

Torres-Rouff, C., & Knudson, K. J. (2017). Integrating identities: An innovative bioarchaeological and biogeochemical approach to analyzing the multiplicity of identities in the mortuary record. *Current Anthropology* 58(3): 381–409. doi:10.1086/692026

Toyne, J. M. (2018). A childhood of violence: A bioarchaeological comparison of mass death assemblages from ancient Peru. In: Beauchesne, P. & Agarwal, S. C. (Eds.) *Children and Childhood in Bioarchaeology*, pp. 171–206. University Press of Florida: Gainesville, FL.

Trigger, B. G. (1999). Shang political organization: A comparative approach. *Journal of East Asian Archaeology* 1(1–4): 43–62.

Troughton, J. H., Wells, P. V., & Mooney, H. A. (1974). Photosynthetic mechanisms and paleoecology from carbon isotope ratios in ancient specimens of C4 and CAM plants. *Science* 185(4151): 610–612. doi:10.1126/science.185.4151.610

Tung, T. A. (2007). Trauma and violence in the Wari empire of the Peruvian Andes: warfare, raids, and ritual fights. *American Journal of Physical Anthropology* 133(3): 941–956. doi:10.1002/ajpa.20565

Tung, T. A. (2008). Dismembering bodies for display: a bioarchaeological study of trophy heads from the Wari site of Conchopata, Peru. *American Journal of Physical Anthropology* 136(3): 294–308. doi:10.1002/ajpa.20812

Tung, T. A. (2012). *Violence, Ritual, and the Wari Empire: A Social Bioarchaeology of Imperialism in the Ancient Andes*. University Press of Florida: Gainesville, FL.

Tung, T. A. (2014). Agency,'Til death do us part? Inquiring about the agency of dead bodies from the ancient Andes. *Cambridge Archaeological Journal* 24(3): 437–452. doi:10.1017/S0959774314000614

Turner, C. G., Scott, R., & Nichol, C. (1991). Scoring procedures for key morphological traits of the permanent dentition: Arizona State University dental anthropology system. In: Kelley, M., & Larsen, C. S. (Eds.) *Advances in Dental Anthropology*, pp. 13–31. Willey-Liss, Inc: New York, NY.

Tylor, E. B. (2005[1861]). *Anahuac Or Mexico And The Mexicans, Ancient And Modern*. Lightening Source Incorporated.

Ubelaker, D. H. (1989). The estimation of age at death from immature human bone. In: Iscan, M. Y. (Ed.) *Age Markers in the Human Skeleton*, pp. 55–70. Charles C. Thomas: Springfield, IL.

Ubelaker, D. H., & Newson, L. A. (2002). Patterns of health and nutrition in prehistoric and historic Ecuador. In: Rose, J. C. & Steckel, R. H. (Eds.), *The Backbone of History: Health and Nutrition in the Western Hemisphere*, pp. 343–375. Cambridge University Press: Cambridge.

Valentine, B., Kamenov, G. D., & Krigbaum, J. (2008). Reconstructing Neolithic groups in Sarawak, Malaysia through lead and strontium isotope analysis. *Journal of Archaeological Science* 35(6): 1463–1473. doi:10.1016/j.jas.2007.10.016

van Kessel, J. (2001). El ritual mortuorio de los aymara de Tarapacá como vivencia y crianza de la vida. *Chungara* 33:221–234. doi:10.4067/S0717-73562001000200006

Van Vleet, K. E. (2009). *Performing Kinship: Narrative, Gender, and the Intimacies of Power in the Andes*. University of Texas Press: Austin, TX.

Vazquez de Arthur, A. (2018). Semiotic portraits: Expressions of communal identity in Wari faceneck vessels. In: Tiesler, V. & Lozada, M. C. (Eds.) *Social Skins of the Head: Body Beliefs and Ritual in Ancient Mesoamerica and the Andes*, pp. 253–268.: University of New Mexico Press: Albuquerque, NM.

Velasco, M. C. (2018). Ethnogenesis and social difference in the Andean Late Intermediate Period (AD 1100–1450): a bioarchaeological study of cranial modification in the Colca Valley, Peru. *Current Anthropology* 59(1): 98–106. doi:10.1086/695986

Wakely, J. (1996). Limits to interpretation of skeletal trauma—two case studies from Medieval Abingdon, England. *International Journal of Osteoarchaeology* 6(1): 76–83. doi:10.1002/(SICI)1099-1212(199601)6:1<76::AID-OA233>3.0.CO;2-H

Waldron, H. A., Khera, A., Walker, G., Wibberly, G., Green, C. J. S. (1979). Lead concentrations in bones and soil. *Journal of Archaeological Science* 6: 295–298. doi:10.1016/0305-4403(79)90008-6

Waldron, T. (2019). Joint disease. In: Buikstra, J. E. (Ed.) *Ortner's Identification of Pathological Conditions in Human Skeletal Remains*, 3rd edition, pp. 719–748. Academic Press: New York, NY.

Walker, P. L. (1986). Porotic hyperostosis in a marine-dependent California Indian population. *American Journal of Physical Anthropology* 69(3): 345–354. doi:10.1002/ajpa.1330690307

Walker, P. L. (1997). Wife beating, boxing, and broken noses: Skeletal evidence for the cultural patterning of violence. In: Martin, D. L. & Frayer, D. W. (Eds.) *Troubled Times: Violence and Warfare in the Past*, pp. 145–180. Gordan and Breach Publishers, Amsterdam.

Walker, P. L. (2001). A bioarchaeological perspective on the history of violence. *Annual Review of Anthropology* 30(1): 573–596. doi:10.1146/annurev.anthro.30.1.573

Walker, P. L. (2008). Bioarchaeological ethics: a historical perspective on the value of human remains. In: Katzenberg, M. & Saunders, S. (Eds.) *Biological Anthropology of the Human Skeleton*, 2nd edition, pp. 3–39. Wiley-Liss, Wilmington DE.

Walker, P. L., Bathurst, R. R., Richman, R., Gjerdrum, T., & Andrushko, V. A. (2009). The causes of porotic hyperostosis and cribra orbitalia: A reappraisal of the iron-deficiency-anemia hypothesis. *American Journal of Physical Anthropology* 139(2), 109–125. doi:10.1002/ajpa.21031

Walrath, D. (2017). Bones, biases, and birth. In: Agarwal, S. C. & Wesp, J. K. (Eds.) *Exploring Sex and Gender in Bioarchaeology*, pp. 15–39. University of New Mexico Press: Albuquerque, NM.

Wang, L. Y., & Marwick, B. (2020). Standardization of ceramic shape: A case study of Iron Age pottery from northeastern Taiwan. *Journal of Archaeological Science: Reports* 33: 102554. doi:10.1016/j.jasrep.2020.102554

Watson, J. T., & Haas, R. (2017). Dental evidence for wild tuber processing among Titicaca Basin foragers 7000 ybp. *American Journal of Physical Anthropology* 164(1): 117–130. doi:10.1002/ajpa.23261

Webster, G. (1990). Labor control and emergent stratification in prehistoric Europe. *Current Anthropology* 31: 337–366. doi:10.1086/203848

Weide, D. M., Fritz, S. C., Hastorf, C. A., Bruno, M. C., Baker, P. A., Guedron, S., & Salenbien, W. (2017). A~ 6000 yr diatom record of mid-to late Holocene fluctuations in the level of Lago Wiñaymarca, Lake Titicaca (Peru/Bolivia). *Quaternary Research* 88(2): 179–192. doi:10.1017/qua.2017.49

Wernke, S. A. (2007). Negotiating community and landscape in the Peruvian Andes: A transconquest view. *American Anthropologist* 109(1): 130–152. doi:10.1525/aa.2007.109.1.130

Wernke, S. A. (2012). Spatial network analysis of a terminal prehispanic and early colonial settlement in highland Peru. *Journal of Archaeological Science* 39(4): 1111–1122. doi:10.1016/j.jas.2011.12.014

Wheeler, S. M., Williams, L., Beauchesne, P., & Dupras, T. L. (2013). Shattered lives and broken childhoods: Evidence of physical child abuse in ancient Egypt. *International Journal of Paleopathology* 3(2): 71–82. doi:10.1016/j.ijpp.2013.03.009

Whitehead, N. L. (2005). War and violence as cultural expression. *Anthropology News* 46(5): 23–26. doi:10.1525/an.2005.46.5.23.1

Williams, J. S., & Murphy, M. S. (2013). Living and dying as subjects of the Inca Empire: Adult diet and health at Puruchuco-Huaquerones, Peru. *Journal of Anthropological Archaeology* 32(2): 165–179. doi:10.1016/j.jaa.2013.01.001

Wilson, J. J. (2014). Paradox and promise: Research on the role of recent advances in paleodemography and paleoepidemiology to the study of "health" in Precolumbian societies. *American Journal of Physical Anthropology* 155(2): 268–280. doi:10.1002/ajpa.22601

Winckelmann, J. J. (1850). *The history of ancient art among the Greeks* (Vol. 2). John Chapman: London.

Wood, J. W., Milner, G. R., Harpending, H. C., & Weiss, K. M. (1992). The Osteological Paradox: Problems of Inferring Prehistoric Health from Skeletal Samples. *Current Anthropology.* 33: 343–370. doi:10.1086/204084

Worne, H., Cobb, C. R., Vidoli, G., & Steadman, D. W. (2012). The Space of War: Connecting Geophysical Landscapes with Skeletal Evidence of Warfare-Related Trauma. In: Martin, D. E., Harrod, R. P. & Pérez, V. R. (eds.) *The Bioarchaeology of Violence*, pp. 141–159. University Press of Florida: Gainesville, FL.

Yaeger, J. & Canuto, M. A. (Eds). (2000). Introducing an Archaeology of Communities. In: Canuto, M. A. & Yager J. (Eds.) *The Archaeology of Communities: A New World Perspective*, pp. 1–15. Routledge: New York, NY.

Zhang, H., Merrett, D. C., Jing, Z., Tang, J., He, Y., Yue, H., ... & Yang, D. Y. (2017). Osteoarthritis, labour division, and occupational specialization of the Late Shang China-insights from Yinxu (ca. 1250–1046 BC). *PloS One* 12(5): e0176329. doi:10.1371/journal.pone.0176329

Zuckerman, M. K., Kamnikar, K. R., Mathena, S. A., Crandall, J. J., & Martin, D. L. (2014). Recovering the 'body politic': A relational ethics of meaning for bioarchaeology. *Cambridge Archaeological Journal* 24(3): 513–522. doi: http://dx.doi.org/10.1017/S0959774314000766

Index

Note: Page numbers in **bold** indicate tables; those in *italics* indicate figures.

access to resources 7, 8, 14, 52, 70, 81, 83
adolescence 14, **33**, 34, 50, 60, 63, 65, 79
adulthood 33, 39
age **33**, 34, 38, 42, 48, 50, 52, 63; at-death 32–3, 44, 53; of rock 60
agriculture 4, 81, 88; incipient 87; raised field 86; *see also* subsistence strategies
Alca 24
alpaca *see* camelids
amaranths 40, 47
anarchy 4–6, 14, 83, 91
ancestor 3, 26, 52, 58, 84–5, 90
ancestry 11, 57, 84
Andes 1, 19, 48, 58–9, 65, 66; geology of 61, 64; ritual in the 84–5; violence in the 87–8
annular modification 68–9
architecture 17, 55, 85–7, 90
Aymara 85

biodistance analysis 11, 58–9, 61–4
biomechanical force 11, 38
body modification 12–13, 88

camelids 18–21, 23, 30, 47–8, 51, 82
canihua 20
carbon 10, 39–40, 44, **46**, 47, 50–1, 53–4
ceramics 3, 6, 19, 26, 29
Ch'isi *25*, 27, **28**, 29, 55, 62, **63**
chicha 52, 85

childhood 32–3, 37, 39, 60, 63, 65
children 39, 67, 84–5
Chile 64
Chiripa 20–1, 24, 25
Chivay 24
Chucuito 15–16
climate change 15, 89–90
coercion 4–5, 24, 86, 91
coercive control *see* coercion
colony 12, 60
community; (bio)archaeology of 7–14, 90–2; descendant 7; imagined 3; natural 3, 11, 59
competition 4, 5, 14, 70, 81–3, 87, 89–91
conflict 6, 13–14, 70–1, 86–8; face to face/interpersonal 14, 70, 74, 77–9; large-scale 13, 69–70, 87–8
cooperation 4, 6, 14, 83–4, 86, 90–1
Copacabana *see* Copacabana Peninsula
Copacabana Peninsula 1, 2, 7, 35, 40, 67, 79, 82–3, 91; agriculture on 86; archaeology of 24, 27–31; climate change on 15, 89; ecology of 15; geology of 63–5; social organization of 89–90; violence on 80–1, 87–8
corporal punishment 70, 81
cranial modification 13, 65, 66–9, **71**, **72**, **73**, 75, *76*, 77, *78*, 79–84, 87–9
cranial suture closure 32–3
cribra orbitalia (CO) 37, **41**, 42, 49, 52

Index

cultivation *see* domestication
Cundisa 27, **28**, 29, 62, **63**, 83

degenerative joint disease *see* osteoarthritis
dental: biodistance traits 59, 61–2, 65; enamel 37, 60; eruption 32; lesions 8–9; modification 13; strontium 60; wear 32
dentition 10, 32, 39, 62; deciduous 65
diet 8–10, 32, 36, 39–40, 44–8, 50–4, 56, 65, 75; *see also* food
disease 7–9, 36–7, 41, 48, 53, 55–6, 65, 83–4, 88, 89; endemic 82; infectious 48, 51; risk of 8–9, 13, 52, 56, 82, 84, 90; zoonotic 48, 84
domestic abuse *see* corporal punishment
domestication 20–3; of camelids 18; plant 51
drought 24, 55, 80–1, 87, 90

Early Horizon (EH) 2, 17, 20, 22–8, 62, 63, 81, 83–7, 88, 90; burials 29, 30, 33–6; cranial modification 71, 72, 75–7, 80; disease, labor and diet 41, 44, 46–53, 56; strontium 63–5; trauma 71, 72, 75–7, 80
Early Intermediate Period (EIP) 2, 17, 24–7, 84–90; burials 27, 29–31, 33–5; cranial modification 71, 72, 77–80; disease, labor and diet 41, 44, 46, 47, 52–6; strontium 63–5; trauma 71, 72, 77–81, 89
eburnation 38, 42, *54*
endogamy *see* relationships, endogamous
erect modification 67, 68, 69, **71**, 72, 73, 75, 76, 77, 78, 82, 83
ethnic: affiliation 67; exclusion 89; group 10, 13, 66–8, 84; multi- 80; neighborhood 10, 88

family 11, 14, 57–9, 64–5, 83–5, 90; *see also* kinship
fertility 26, 33, 55

fissioning 22, 24
food 2, 9–11, 19, 21, 26, 29, 36, 48, 52, 54, 59, 60, 81, 84, 86, 88, 90; *see also* diet
foraging 19–20, 22, 44, 46–8, 51, 86, 91
fracture 14, 39, 70–3, 74, 75, 76, 77, 78, 79, 84; Colles' 71, 78, 79; parry 71, 74

gender 6, 8, 13, 34, 88, 89

hat-brim line 70, 77
head 25–7, 66; modified 12, 67, 68, 69, 77, 80, 81; trauma to the 70–1, 77; trophy 87
health *see* disease
heterarchy 4–6, 14, 83, 88–9
hierarchy 4–6, 8, 14, 24, 26, 65, 75, 82, 85, 88–91
hormones 33–4, 38
horticulture 21–2, 51; *see also* subsistence strategies

iconography 3, 6, 19, 25–6, 84, 87, 90
identity 2, 14, 26, 65, 74, 75, 84, 85; collective 1, 57–8; local 12, 59; markers of 12–13, 57, 66–8, 79, 81, 83, 88; *see also* in-group
immune system 9, 37, 55
inequality 5, 14, 34, 55, 69, 87, 89–91
infants 11, **33**, 58, 67, 84–5
in-group 1, 6, 14, 57, 66–7, 75, 83
Initial Period **17**, 20–2, 25
Inka 12, **17**, 23, 59, 85
isotopes 7, 35; stable 10, 39–40, **46**, 47, 50–1, 53–5; strontium 12, 60, 61, 63, 64, 65, 77

juveniles 31, **33**, 41, 42, 48, 49, 53, 54–5, 63, 65, 67, 75, 76, 77, 79, 84–5; camelids 21

Kenasfena 27, **28**, 29, *31*, 83
kinship 1, 2, 11, 57–9, 64–5, 84–6, 88; biological 58, 64, 84; fictive 57, 59

labor 2, 7, 9–12, 14, 23, 35, 36, 38–9, 50, 52, 55, 59, 75, 82, 84, 86–91
Lake Titicaca 15, *16*; *see also* Titicaca Basin
linear enamel hypoplasia (LEH) 37–8, **41**, *42*, *49*, 51
llama *see* camelids

maize 22, 40, 47, 51, 52, 84, 85
marriage 57, 58; *see also* family; kinship
migration 2, 14, 65, 77; *see also* mobility
mobility 7, 11–12, 59–61, 64, 89
Moquegua Valley 64
Muruqullu 27, **28**, 29, *30*, 55, 62, **63**, 65, 82, 83

nitrogen 10, 39–40, 44, **46**, 47, 53
nonlocal 63–5, 77; *see also* migration
nonmetric dental variation *see* dental, biodistance traits
nutrition 8–9, 14, 37, 48, 51, 88; deficiencies 37, 42; mal- 9, 35, 36, 37, 40, 48, 51, 55, 70, 84, 90

oblique modification 68, 69, **71**, *72*, *75*, *76*, 77, *78*, *79*, 80, 83
obsidian 24
osteoarthritis 10–11, 38–9, 42–3, **44**, *45*, **46**, 48, *50*, 52, 53, *54*, 56, 82
osteological paradox 8
osteomyelitis 37, **41**, *42*, *43*, *49*, 52, 53
out-group 1, 66–7

parasites 37, 48; *see also* disease, zoonotic
pathogen 9, 36, 48, 51; *see also* disease, infectious
periosteal reactions 36–7, **41**, *42*, *43*, *49*, 51, 52, *53*, 56
Peru 15, 20–1, 24, 30, *61*, 64, 83
phenotype 11, 58, 65, 82
porosity 36, 38, 39, 42; *see also* cribra orbitalia; porotic hyperostosis
porotic hyperostosis (PH) 37, **41**, *42*, *43*, *49*, 52, *53*, 56

potato 20, 59
Preceramic Period 2, **17**, 19–20, 27, 82–4, 90; burials **28**, 29, 31, 33–6; cranial modification **71**, **72**, *73*, *74*, *75*; disease, labor and diet 40, **41**, 42, *43–5*, **46**, 47, 48, 50, 52, 56; strontium 62–5; trauma **71**, **72**, *73*, *74*, *75*, 80
protein 10, 39–40, 46–8, 53–6, 87
Pukara 87
puna 22

Qhot'a Pata 27, **28**, 30
Qopakati 27, **28**, 30–1, 61, 63
quinoa 20, 22

relationships 1, 3–7, 13, 24, 33, 36, 57–9, 67, 77, 84–6, 88–9, 91; endogamous 58, 65; genetic 11, 58, 65, 88; geographic 12, 59–60, 65; reciprocal 22; reproductive 11, 58; ritual 26, 84
ritual 9–10, 24–7, 55, 70, 84–8; architecture 55; fights 13; goods 25, 26, 29–32; knowledge 4; space 6, 9

Schmorl's nodes 39, 42–3, *45*, *50*, 53
sedentary settlements 4, 20, 21, 24, 26, 51–2, 80, 84, 86
sedentism *see* sedentary settlements
sex 32–4, **35**, 38, 42, 43, 49, 50, 52, 53, 55, 63, 65, 71, 74–7, 88, 89; dimorphism 33; linked traits 34, 62
social class 5, 8, 67, 70, 85; *see also* inequality
social networks 5, 24, *55*, 57
starvation *see* malnutrition
stelae 25–7, 30, 31
Straits of Tiquina 15, 30
stress 7–9, 35–43, 55–6, 84, 86, 88; bodily 38, 48–53, 55, 84; chronic 9, 37; environmental 13, 24, 70; mechanical 38; nutritional 51; psychosocial 8; systemic 14
strontium 12, 35, 60–1, 63–5, 77; baselines 60, *61*; signatures 12, 61, 63, 64

Index

subsistence strategies 3, 8, 16, 19–22, 26, 35, 56, 58, 81

tabular modification 68–9
Taraco 26, 87
Taraco Peninsula 52, 54, 85
Tawa Qeñani 27, **28**, 31, 62, 63
temple 25, 26, 27, 29–31, 52, 83–7, 90; domains 23
terraces 23, 24, 54, 84, 86, 90
territory 66, 70, 80, 83, 87–8
Titicaca Basin 1, 2, 11–12, 15, *16*, **17**, 36, 46–7, 52, 59, 63, 64, 83, 85, 90; archaeology of 19–27; birds of 18; ecology of 15–18; fish of 18, 47, 48; geology of 60–1, 64; mammals of 18–19, 47
Tiwanaku 17, 19, 88–9
top-down vertical control *see* hierarchy

trade 11–12, 21, 22, 24, 59, 84; long-distance 23–4, 26, 60, 64
trauma 7, 13–14, 35, 38, 39, 48, 65, 67, 70, **71**, **72**, **73**, 74–7, 80–4, 87–90; antemortem 72, 74, *78*, 79; blunt force 83; perimortem 75, 76, 78–9; sharp force 74, 75
trepanation 77–8; *see also* conflict

villages *see* sedentary settlements
violence 2, 8, 13–14, 66–7, 69–71, 74, 77, 79, 80–4, 86–91; abnormal 13, 70, 83; normalized 13, 70, 79, 88; *see also* conflict

war *see* conflict, large-scale
Wiñaymarka 2, 15–16, 47–8

Yaya-Mama Project 27
Yaya-Mama Religious Tradition 17, 25–7, 29–31, 83–7, 90

For Product Safety Concerns and Information please contact our EU representative GPSR@taylorandfrancis.com
Taylor & Francis Verlag GmbH, Kaufingerstraße 24, 80331 München, Germany